The
Immoral
Christian

Dr. Kevin L. Thomas

DEDICATION

To my loving wife, Melissa, who lived with my
obsession about this work, read it, edited it, believed
in me, and was a constant source of strength and
encouragement. I love you!

To the people who courageously shared their stories
with me and trusted me to share them with you. You
are my heroes!

To the 31 million Americans and millions more
worldwide who have left the church because of the
church. God treasures you, and so do I.

CONTENTS

ACKNOWLEDGMENTS

To my church family at Forest Lake United Methodist Church who helped me to shape these ideas through weekly book studies. Your unconditional love for God and people gives me hope for the future of the church.

PART ONE:

THE FALLACY OF MORALITY

1 PARADOX

The immoral Christian—it's a paradox, right? For many, the two words are mutually exclusive. By definition, Christians must also be moral, or so I thought for years. Now, I wonder. What if obsession with rules has distracted us from the heart of Christianity? What if trying to be good is not the key to following Christ? Could it be that morality is actually an obstacle to grace?

I ask that you suspend judgement until you've read the pages of this book. Maybe you won't change your mind. Maybe these chapters will cause you to question my Christianity. But, just maybe we will discover a better way forward, a way that invites all to join and find life.

Very often morality defines Christianity. Like many of you, church youth groups were an important part of my teenage years. I remember many discussions focusing on the question, "What does it mean to be a Christian?" Youth members inevitably answered with a predictable list of "don'ts." Don't lie! Don't steal! Don't skip church! Don't drink! Don't cuss! Don't do drugs! Don't think about the opposite sex! Heaven forbid—don't have premarital sex! For many, these "don't" rules defined Christianity. Their way of thinking leads to a larger question, "How did we arrive at this understanding?"

Largely, I'm afraid; youth got their opinions of the faith from the church. After listening with a critical ear to the messages that we pastors, youth directors, Sunday school teachers, and parents are preaching, I discovered that many of us have been feeding a steady diet of moralism to the next generation. To be fair, we did it out of genuine concern. Teen alcoholism, teen pregnancy, sexually transmitted infections, and drug addiction are real dangers. We want to protect our kids. I understand the temptation to use threats of hell fire to try to keep our kids safe from the perilous world in which they live.

I understand, but I no longer approve. Our efforts to scare youth into healthy behavior have been counterproductive. Our scary stories about sex, drugs, and Rock 'n' Roll only seem to encourage those behaviors, especially after an experiment or two with them seems to prove the adults wrong. After all, for all their dangers, most of the "don'ts" are a lot of fun! Once youth discover the joy they find in adult's lists of evils, they will likely reject the whole system of morality that tried to protect them from those very "evils" in the first place. Not only is our "don'ts" list ineffective, defining Christianity in terms of morality leads to one of two disastrous outcomes: arrogance or despair.

First, those teens who actually manage to navigate their culture strictly adhering to the "don'ts" are likely to put their trust in their good behavior. They assume they are Christian because they follow the rules. This spiritual arrogance deceives them into believing that all is well with their faith. In reality, though, all our good behavior is crap. Paul had just that view of his excellent behavior. "What is more, I consider everything a loss because of the surpassing worth of knowing Christ Jesus my Lord, for whose sake I have lost all things. I consider them *garbage*, that I may gain Christ" (Philippians 3:8 emphasis added). Garbage, or in the King James Version dung—crap, that's how our best behavior adds up. I am deeply concerned about countless numbers of people who have grown up thinking their eternity is safe because they didn't have sexual intercourse before marriage.

The second danger of a moralistic view of the faith is that it condemns those who have failed. It sends those who have done the "don'ts" to hell. I have seen too many teens walk away from youth groups because they've messed up. They went out to a party and got drunk. Maybe they decided to go "all the way" with a boyfriend or girlfriend. According to one report, 88% of teens who take the purity pledge break it before marriage (Altman). There is simply no place for such failures in a faith dictated by the "don'ts." There's very little good news for those who have already done the "don'ts"—no grace, just despair. For both those who have followed the rules and for those who haven't, moralism overlooks the fact that we are saved only by grace (Ephesians 2:8-9). Our relationship with Christ is a gift only He can offer, and the offer is independent of our behavior, good or bad.

What is true among youth groups is consistent across every spectrum of American culture. "The fact that more than three out of every five churchgoing Christians equate Christianity with a list of moral rules to be followed is troubling — especially the fact that they agreed this is 'the most important' priority of following Jesus" (Barna 80). Personal experience confirms Barna's research. A senior citizen told me that he would come to church when he got his life in order. Middle aged folks stay away because they realize their lifestyles don't match the expectations of legalistic churches. A young adult recently shared with me that she and her husband had to "work up the courage" to attend church. We've created the illusion that acting within certain religious norms of behavior automatically includes people in the Christian family. We've communicated the converse as well, that for those who fall outside of the norms, there is no room in the family. A couple of years ago, I was privileged to hear a young woman's powerful testimony. In front of a large gathering of church folks, she courageously testified about the awesome way that God transformed her life. After sharing, she came down off the stage to be greeted by a church person with, "I can't believe you were up there with all those tattoos." Who knew that a little ink could blind people to the incredible work of an almighty God! Unfortunately, that exchange is symptomatic of our times. Too many have exchanged the riches of glory for a few rules, and we can't even be certain that the rules are right. We deceived ourselves into believing that our morals are based on timeless principles.

In reality, we more often evaluate Christian spirituality in terms of cultural norms of morality, standards that change with the generations. It's easy to assume the state of a person's soul based on the normality of his or her behavior. But, what if our norms are wrong? Throughout most of my life, very few have seriously questioned the sanctity of Christian marriage. It is the assumed way of relating in most churches to the exclusion of all other relationships. In fact, I've known many single people who felt that their spirituality was treated as substandard because of their singleness. Our culture has venerated the Christian family unit above all else, including the church. Family time is an acceptable excuse for avoiding virtually any Christian calling. Certainly, a solid marriage is sufficient evidence of deep Christian spirituality. Not if you ask the Apostle Paul. According to him, "Now to the unmarried and the widows I say: It is good for them to stay unmarried, as I do. But if they cannot control themselves, they should marry, for it is better to marry than to burn with passion" (I Corinthians 7:8-9). Rather than seeing Christian marriage as a virtue, the Apostle viewed it as a sign of weakness, a necessity for those who can't control themselves! Marriage was simply a way to avoid sexual sin for those Christians who weren't strong enough to remain celibate. St. Augustine was even stronger in opposing marriage, rejecting it altogether. We'll come back to marriage in chapter two.

In similar fashion, many traditions today exclude from service anyone who is divorced. This exclusion is for life! Oddly enough, in the 8th Century, priests were allowed to have both multiple wives and concubines (Manning 46). In the 1980's many of us questioned the faith of those who consumed alcohol, an attitude that prompted many covert trips to the liquor store for church members. Prior to 1800, alcohol simply wasn't an issue. It only became an issue in response to political pressures which we'll cover in chapter five.

The above examples point to an obvious weakness in moralism. We humans have a view of history that's limited to about 70 years. Our narrow view causes us to think that what is important to us must have always been important. We prefer to think that the Apostles would agree with us on all our opinions of right and wrong. The reality is that the rules have changed—a lot.

The devout people I know would be in serious trouble in 17th and 18th Century America. I know that I wouldn't make the grade. Following are a few examples of early American Christian morality. For an unexcused church absence, the offender could be fined a pound of tobacco. (That example alone illustrates an odd conflict of values across the centuries. It exhibits strictness on church attendance that shocks along with permissiveness towards tobacco that would surprise many in today's church.) Continued absences incurred an even stricter sentence. A month out of church could result in ten lashes. Additionally, outlawed on Sunday were ordinary labor, business, trade, recreation, amusements, shooting, fishing, sporting, and playing. There went my weekend! The standards of the American State Papers seem extreme even to the most upstanding among us: "whosoever shall profane the Lords-day, by doing unnecessary servile work, by unnecessary [travailing], or by sports and recreations, he or they that so transgress, shall forfeit for every such default forty shillings, or be [publickly] whipt: But if it clearly appear that the sin was proudly, presumptuously and with a high hand committed, against the known Command and Authority of the blessed God, such a person therein despising and reproaching the Lord, shall he put to death or grievously punished at the Judgement of the Court" (Blakley 37).

To us, these examples seem archaic and extreme, and perhaps they are. But, their absurdity proves the point. There are extreme variances in interpretation of Christian morality across the centuries. It is blatantly arrogant to assume that out of 2000 years, we are the ones who are right. These examples suggest that cultural morality might not be the best barometer for Christian spirituality.

The consideration of an immoral Christian is significant and relevant to our time. The association of morality with Christianity is damaging to the cause of Christ. We turn people away from the church over issues that are not central to the Gospel. In my ministry, I have encountered horror stories of people who have felt the sting of a church door slammed in their faces. A woman in her fifties, still carrying the emotional scars, shared a troubling story with me. As a teenage girl, dressed in blue jeans, she went with a friend to church on Sunday night. The morally upstanding church folks sent her away because of her wardrobe transgression. The emotional trauma was so severe that it took this woman 35 years to enter a church. In fact, it was only when she started attending a worship service held in her apartment complex that she began to hear the Good News. Then, there's the story of the teenage girl who faithfully played piano for her church's worship service until she got pregnant. The leadership of her church forced her to give up her service in worship. Who knew that pregnancy causes you to forget how to play the piano? By the way, pregnancy has never been a sin. How conveniently we ignore the sexual activity of our teens until they get pregnant! I have seen cold receptions in the church for people of different races, people who have tattoos, or too many piercings. (I don't know who gets to decide the appropriate number.) Sadly, I've seen people walk away from a church they love for fear that they might have to worship in the same building with people of a different sexual orientation. Our arbitrary moral standards routinely obstruct entrance into the kingdom of God. These and many other examples beg the questions, "Whose entrance to the kingdom of God is being obstructed?—Theirs or ours?"

Not only do we arbitrarily exclude individuals from Christ's love for their "bad behavior," but we also encourage people to be moral without teaching them to follow Christ. Take the "True Love Waits" pledge, attend "See You at the Polls" prayer rallies, vote for the right ticket, complain about Supreme Court decisions, and recite "The Lord's Prayer" at Friday night football games, and you are securely on the inside with the church crowd. "A leading Puritan divine, the Rev. John Cotton, went so far as to maintain that hypocrites who merely conform to the church rules without inner conviction could still be useful church members" (Rothbard 2). Such attitudes might serve the church, but they do not serve the people God loves. Good behavior gives us the opportunity to feel safe without following Jesus, the one who said, "love your enemies and pray for those who persecute you, that you may be children of your Father in heaven" (Matthew 5:44-45b). It's safer to be moral than to really follow the one who said, "Do not store up for yourselves treasures on earth, where moths and vermin destroy, and where thieves break in and steal" (Matthew 6:19). Was Jesus speaking to today's church when He said, "You have let go of the commands of God and are holding on to human traditions" (Mark 7:8 NIV)?

Even those within the fold are in danger if they dare to violate the moral standards of the group. One of the saddest things in my 30 years as a pastor is witnessing people struggling through personal pain in isolation. When marriages are falling apart, kids are in trouble, or drugs or alcohol are destroying people's lives, people hide those struggles from their churches. What a sad commentary! When life is at its worst, the church should be a source of strength. Because of moralism, we've turned it into a place of condemnation.

Pope Francis seems to understand the danger of our present situation. In October 2013, he shared the following comments in a homily on Radio Vatican.

The faith passes, so to speak, through a distiller and becomes ideology. And ideology does not beckon [people]. In ideologies there is not Jesus: his tenderness, his love, his meekness. And ideologies are rigid, always. Of every sign: rigid. And when a Christian becomes a disciple of the ideology, he has lost the faith: he is no longer a disciple of Jesus, he is a disciple of this attitude of thought... For this reason Jesus said to them: 'You have taken away the key of knowledge.' The knowledge of Jesus is transformed into an ideological and also moralistic knowledge, because these close the door with many requirements.

The faith becomes ideology and ideology frightens, ideology chases away the people, distances, distances the people and distances the Church from the people. But it is a serious illness, this of ideological Christians. It is an illness, but it is not new, eh? Already the Apostle John, in his first Letter, spoke of this. Christians who lose the faith and prefer the ideologies. His attitude is: be rigid, moralistic, ethical, but without kindness. This can be the question, no? But why is it that a Christian can become like this? Just one thing: this Christian does not pray. And if there is no prayer, you always close the door.

The key that opens the door to the faith," the Pope added, "is prayer." The Holy Father warned: "When a Christian does not pray, this happens. And his witness is an arrogant witness." He who does not pray is "arrogant, is proud, is sure of himself. He is not humble. He seeks his own advancement." Instead, he said, "when a Christian prays, he is not far from the faith; he speaks with Jesus.

The Pope is right. Preaching against various lifestyles is an effective way to isolate ourselves from those we don't love! We've reached a point in American history when the country is tired of our moralism. The culture doesn't care if we don't like its tattoos, its sexuality, or its profanity. But, that doesn't make the culture our enemy. The church can't blame the culture for disliking our bad ideas. And, the people want more. Spiritual hunger is growing at an exponential rate. It's time for the church to, once again, fall deeply in love with God and with all of our neighbors.

If you're still reading, maybe you agree that the "don'ts" don't get anybody into the kingdom of God. Maybe you're realizing that the church has too often been pickier than God with regards to who we're willing to love. Over the next four chapters, I will continue to expose the fallacy of morality. Chapter two will address the Christian family unit. Chapter three will explore human sexuality. In Chapter four, we'll consider profanity, and in Chapter five we'll take a fresh look at alcohol. Then, in part two, I will lay out a plan for a better way. I will describe a path to Christian living that focuses on prayer and other Christian disciplines. Rather than focusing on moralism and legalism, we will learn to fall more deeply in love with Christ and with our fellow human beings. And, we will learn to trust Christ, not the church, to shape our behavior.

2 THE FOURTH PERSON OF THE TRINITY

"God only created two institutions, the church and the family, and He created the family first."
                    -A popular saying in my early faith development

"Sunday mornings are the loneliest part of my week." The words shocked me as they came out of Sandy's mouth. She was a faithful member, a devout Christ follower. She taught Sunday school and daily served both church and community. Christ was the center of her life. There were plenty of people in our church that adored Sandy. They considered her a valued friend. How could her morning at church be such a negative experience? I asked for more information. The source of Sandy's misery was not the music, the liturgy, or the uncomfortable pews. She didn't complain about the preaching, thankfully, or even the temperature. Sandy is single. "Church is for families," she said, "and every time I come to worship I get the feeling that I just don't fit."

While aware of the needs of Christian singles, I had never consciously thought about the unspoken message they heard from the Church. It never occurred to me that, inadvertently, I had been leaving out those who did not fit the Christian nuclear family mold. Throughout my ministry, I have encouraged strong Christian families, but I had never intentionally meant to leave behind those who did not fit into this box. I never realized that by encouraging strong Christian families I might be sending a hidden message to Christian singles. Specifically, I was accidentally making singles feel excluded from the Church. Because of this accidental message, how many single Christians simply stayed away from worship in order to avoid feeling excluded? Sandy exposed some of my own biases; causing me to reconsider ideas that I had too easily accepted.

"God only created two institutions, the church and the family, and He created the family first." With that over simplified statement, the pastor tried to convince me of the primacy of the Christian family unit, and I bought it. Why wouldn't I? It fit my story—married with children. Throughout most of my life, the acceptable definition of family has been a father, a mother, and some number of children living under one roof. In recent times, the Christian family has been essentially elevated to become the fourth person of the Trinity. All other relationships are treated as secondary at best and sinful at worst. Often, the pain caused by this opinion has led single people, like Sandy, into my study. Some of them were single by choice. Some just hadn't found the right person. Their question is the same. "What good news does the Bible have for us single people?" Without spouse and kids, they didn't feel like full participants in the church. Even those who are married often feel somewhat excluded from church if they don't have kids. My aunt and uncle deeply loved children and wanted to have their own. They were unable to conceive. They lived in a time when adoption was not widely accepted. Both of them carried to their graves the guilt of not achieving the Christian family unit. Traditional families can be a good way to live, but they are not the only way. They are not the best way for everyone, and they are certainly not the only relationships that God blesses.

Of course, the Bible affirms marriage between one man and one woman. The creation stories of Genesis one and two tell of God's creating man and woman. Their union is summed up with, "That is why a man leaves his father and mother and is united to his wife, and they become one flesh" (Genesis 2:24). With the obvious goal of populating a planet, heterosexual marriage only makes sense. Jesus affirms the importance of this union when He adds, "What God has joined together, let no one separate" (Matthew 19:6b). His focus is on not breaking the relationship, a practice that is now morally acceptable in most of our society. Traditional marriage is affirmed again in other places like Ephesians 5:22ff where Paul compares the church to marriage. He compares the role of the wife with that of the church and the role of the husband with that of Christ. This passage is the key source for Christian marriage enrichment seminars across the western world. It is also the justification for violence for too many. Abusive husbands use Paul's instructions to wives to be submissive as an excuse for all manner of inhumane treatment. Selective reading allows those same husbands to ignore verses in the same passage which call on the husband to sacrifice greatly for his wife's well-being. Paul encourages women to respect their husbands and men to love their wives sacrificially. It's good advice. But, then he explains that he is primarily talking about Christ and the church (Ephesians 5:32). If these were the only expressions of marriage in Scripture, we would be forced to conclude that Christian marriage is, in fact, defined as one man and one woman. Popular church culture draws this conclusion.

Old Testament

But, there are other examples of marriage in the Bible. Jacob, the father of the twelve tribes of Israel worked for seven years to earn the right to marry Rachel. On their wedding day, her father tricked Jacob into marrying her older (and physically less pleasing) sister Leah. Upon discovering the deceit, Jacob agrees to work for another seven years to also marry Rachel. Jacob was a bigamist. While Jacob does have his problems, the Bible never condemns or even criticizes him for having two wives.

One common explanation for Jacob's "bad" behavior is that it occurred before the Ten Commandments were given. In short, he's excused because he didn't know any better. That excuse doesn't work for David who had as many as eight wives at a time and up to ten concubines. Through all his relationships, there is no condemnation for adultery. God gave him a complete pass on his sexual escapades provided he played by the cultural rules of the time, which essentially asserted that a man could sleep with as many women as he could support financially. David's polygamist lifestyle is never questioned until he sleeps with Bathsheba, another man's wife. The prohibition against adultery was a rule against stealing another man's wife. David's sin was not against Bathsheba, but against Bathsheba's husband, Uriah. For this act, David was condemned and ultimately lost the throne. This story and others that follow illustrate the fact that sexual morality and misogyny are hopelessly intertwined in scripture. Biblical sexual codes of ethics assume that women are property, and the laws are written to protect their owners: husbands, fathers, and brothers. We'll address this issue more thoroughly in the next chapter.

David's successor to the throne, his son Solomon, continued and expanded on his father's polygamy. Scripture records 700 wives and 300 concubines in Solomon's harem, and still no condemnation. In fact, multiple wives are helpful when your vision is to turn one family into a great nation. Israel needed people, and its marriage customs were adjusted to meet that need rather than some evasive timeless truth. Marriage customs were determined by practical community needs rather than moral code, a theme consistent throughout history and across cultures. In an agrarian economy with high demands for laborers, polygamy is much more common. Fathers needed numerous children to work the land. In this economy, children are an asset, and multiple wives are the quickest route to develop those assets. With the dawn of the Industrial Revolution, men were expected to leave home and work to support the wife and kids. In this economy, children are a financial liability. The more children a man has, the more mouths to feed off his meager paycheck. When men went to factories to work, families shrunk in size. Marriage and family are economically driven.

The book of Esther gives another insight into Old Testament relationships. While the Jews were slaves in Persia, the king divorced his wife. To replace her, the Persians held what can only be described as an ancient series of The Bachelor. Officials gathered all the prettiest women in the land into a group. Night after night, the king slept with a new woman from the group. After their date, the woman was added to the harem. The faithful Jew Mordecai offered his own cousin Esther for the contest, which she won. Esther's ascension to the throne ultimately saved her people. The success of the plan shouldn't obscure the fact that Mordecai pimped out his cousin as a means to an end. The treatment of women as property is simply assumed with no condemnation.

Many in the church argue that monogamous, heterosexual marriage is the only approved relationship. They can't prove it by the Old Testament.

New Testament

For decades, those of us in the church have been grateful that the New Testament clears up the marriage issue. As I already mentioned, Jesus did affirm that a man and woman become one flesh in marriage. So, we married church folks soundly anchor our belief in the superiority of Christian marriage in the New Testament.

The problem is that the New Testament says other things about marriage, too. Jesus lifts up celibacy as a good option.

10 The disciples said to him, "If this is the situation between a husband and wife, it is better

not to marry." 11 Jesus replied, "Not everyone can accept this word, but only those to whom it has been given. 12 For there are eunuchs who were born that way, and there are eunuchs who have been made eunuchs by others—and there are those who choose to live like eunuchs for the sake of the kingdom of heaven. The one who can accept this should accept it" (Matthew 19:10-12).

In this short passage, Jesus makes room at the table for a wider variety of relationships. There are those who simply don't fit the mold of man/woman relationships. Eunuchs are included. Jesus even goes so far as to recommend that those who can live like eunuchs should do so. Celibacy is celebrated as an alternative to marriage. Asexuals have a place in the kingdom! Jesus continues the theme in Luke 20.

"Jesus replied, 'The people of this age marry and are given in marriage. But those who are considered worthy of taking part in the age to come and in the resurrection from the dead will neither marry nor be given in marriage, and they can no longer die; for they are like the angels. They are God's children, since they are children of the resurrection'" (34-36).

Jesus expects that his followers will include people in a variety of relationships. Marriage is not the only way of relating for Christians. It is not even the preferred method. And, in the end, it will pass away with the rest of the things of this world.

As we discussed in chapter one, Paul (the same guy who wrote the Ephesians 5 text about marriage), actually recommended celibacy as superior to marriage. "Now to the unmarried and the widows I say: It is good for them to stay unmarried, as I do.

But if they cannot control themselves, they should marry, for it is better to marry than to burn with passion" (I Corinthians 7:8-9). For him, marriage was evidence of weakness and a distraction from following God. He considered it an appropriate way to cope with sexual urges that couldn't be suppressed by will, alone. Far from being the most important institution created by God, the New Testament and the early church tended to give it second position at best. The early church would do little to clarify the issue.

Church History

The first 200 years of Christianity saw wildly different views of marriage ranging from celibacy to free love. Neither extreme was fully condemned, and marriage was not elevated as the preferred cultural norm.

The Encratists called for complete celibacy, even in marriage. In their view, similar to Paul's, sex and marriage are distractions that impede our devotion to God. St. Augustine continues their logic in asserting that marriage is inferior to celibacy. It is not coincidence that Augustine's beliefs were born out of his own sexually troubled life. Embedded in his profound teachings were his own sexual struggles, and the church has difficulty distinguishing between his sound orthodoxy and his unhealthy sexuality. In the Apocryphal Acts of the Apostles, St. Thomas demonstrated the profoundly negative view of marriage in early Christian circles when he interrupted a married couple on their wedding night with these words.

Know that if you refrain from this filthy

intercourse you become temples holy and pure, being released from afflictions and troubles, known and unknown, and you will not be involved in the cares of life and of children, whose end is destruction. But if you get many children, for their sakes you become grasping and avaricious, plundering orphans and deceiving widows, and by doing this you subject yourselves to most grievous punishments... But if you obey and preserve your souls pure to God, there will be born to you living children, untouched by these hurtful things, and you will be without care, spending an untroubled life, free from grief and care, looking forward to receive that incorruptible and true marriage, and you will enter as groomsmen into that bridal chamber full of immortality and light (Price 127).

These early Christians were more opponents than fans of the Christian family unit.

Another theologian who was writing at the time of St. Augustine equally opposed marriage, but on entirely different grounds. Epiphanes draws on the tradition of the early church in having all things in common. He extends that belief to include marriage and sexuality. Private possession of anything, including wives, gives opportunity for greed and envy to take root. By sharing everything, Epiphanes believed that people could return to the perfect state of the Creation. Monogamy prevents the sharing of God's good gifts.

But particularity of the laws cut up and destroyed the sharing decreed by the divine law... The idea of 'mine' and 'thine' was introduced by the laws so that the earth and wealth were no longer put to common use and not even marriage... God made all things for man to be in common; he brought female to be in common with male and in the same way united all animals. He thus shows righteousness to consist in sharing, together with equality. But, those who have been born in this way have denied the sharing that brought about their birth and say, "Let him who has taken one woman keep her," whereas in fact a alike can share her just as the other animals have shown (Price 128).

For Epiphanes, human law interfered with the divine order. He considered monogamy a type of coveting and free love as one means of returning to paradise.

As contrasting as these two viewpoints are, they actually share some common threads. Both are anchored in scripture. They agree that traditional marriage can interfere with Christian faith. Distrust or abhorrence of physical desire is common to both. Encratists and Epiphanes both try to supersede Old Testament Law, a theme common to the Gospels and to Paul. Both try to surpass the Law by offering something better than marriage.

The centuries before the Nicene Creed, our first widely accepted statement of faith, would not provide clarity on Christian marriage. The following years would not do much better.

Nicene Creed to Pope Innocent II

Through four ecumenical councils, the church attempted to define orthodox Christianity. The best minds of the times came together to debate exactly who Jesus is, God or man or some combination. They argued about the Holy Spirit and whether he proceeds from the Father and the Son or just from the Father. They made the distinction that Jesus was begotten, not made, coeternal with the Father. These exhaustive debates continued over a couple hundred years in an effort to accurately and faithfully define Christianity. The Nicene Creed became the standard by which orthodox Christianity was judged. Not included in their debates: marriage, sexuality, or any other moral concerns. Even though sex and marriage were popular topics for discussion, neither rose to the level of creedal concerns for early church leaders.

While ecumenical councils wrestled with orthodoxy, asceticism became popular with various Christian groups. In an effort to draw closer to God, people denied themselves of most worldly pleasures including sexual relationships. Ascetics chose lives of solitude and poverty. Some even punished their bodies physically through self-flagellation. Asceticism was voluntary as a means of striving for God. Even the monastics who practiced this lifestyle never attempted to require celibacy of all Christians.

In fact, priests generally rejected the ascetic lifestyle. For the first 1000 years of the church both polygamy and concubinage were common in the priesthood. These practices only became problematic when the church began to amass wealth which the sons of priests could legally inherit. A polygamous priesthood created far too many heirs for Rome's comfort. In an effort to secure church property, Pope Pelagius I declared that all priests must sign agreements that their sons could not inherit property (Makuntima 32). (Daughters had no right to inheritance.) Not satisfied with his predecessor's actions, in AD 1022, Pope Benedict VIII banned priests from marrying or taking concubines

(Schneider). Priests who were married before ordination were allowed to keep their wives. Not surprisingly, many priests married before their ordinations. So, in AD 1139, Pope Innocent II, at the Second Lateran Council, effectively put an end to the issue by annulling all priests' marriages and making celibacy the law (Owen). Still, this was a practical financial decision, not a moral one.

As far as marriage among the laity, the church stayed out of the wedding business for 900 years. "There is no detailed account of a Christian wedding ceremony until the 9th Century, it wasn't until the 12th Century that a priest became involved in the ceremony and not until the 13th Century that he took charge of it" (Signpost 02). Many argue that when the church finally did assume a role in wedding ceremonies it was for financial gain. Sadly, my own denomination now faces almost certain schism over a ritual that the church didn't even perform for almost 1000 years!

The Protestant Reformation

October 31, 1517 marked the beginning of the Protestant Reformation and a monumental shift in western Christianity. It's only during the last 500 years that "Christian marriage" has found its prominence, and it's only in the last 100 years that monogamy has become the primary style of relationship worldwide. "During the seventh session of the Council of Trent in 1547, sacramental marriage became part of canon law" in the Roman Catholic Church (U. S. Catholic). Both Catholic and Protestant churches have affirmed monogamous, heterosexual marriage for most of this period, but there are exceptions. Martin Luther, the man who initiated the Reformation, after much thought gave permission to a church member to marry a second wife. The gentleman in question was a part of a marriage arranged since his childhood. This husband of a wife he didn't choose fell in love with another woman. Luther argued that he could find no scriptural reason to forbid the nuptials (archive.org).

Of course, the debate of the present church surrounds same-sex marriage. We'll look at homosexuality more closely in the next chapter. For now, we must admit that the backdrop for the current debate includes: celibacy, monogamy, polygamy, concubinage, divorce, and misogyny. Regardless of our opinions, the truth is simply not as clear as we wish it were.

Obviously, I've only presented a very broad history of marriage. Many more volumes could be written without exhausting information and points of view. I offer this survey to raise questions about our current understanding of morality and how that understanding might affect the work of the church in the world. My purpose in writing this chapter is not to give preference to polygamy, celibacy, or open marriage, nor is it my design to denigrate heterosexual, monogamous marriage. I am enjoying my thirtieth year of marriage to my only wife, Melissa. For us it works, but I am no longer arrogant enough to force my style of relating on everyone. My desire is to illustrate that neither the Bible nor church history asserts one right way of being in relationship.

3 UNASHAMED

"This is now bone of my bones
and flesh of my flesh;
she shall be called 'woman,'
for she was taken out of man.
That is why a man leaves his father and mother and is
united to his wife, and they become one flesh. Adam and his
wife were both naked, and they felt no shame.
(Genesis 2:25 NIV).

Human sexuality in the Bible begins with this beautiful, poetic, intimate encounter between Adam and Even. Upon meeting one another, they delight in each other's bodies. They enjoy the God-given delight of intercourse. They become one flesh with no shame, no judgment, no guilt. Sex is good, wholesome, holy, a perfect part of a perfect creation.

Ever since their rendezvous, people have tried to regulate the gift of sexuality. The Old Testament provides a long list of laws designed to keep the purity of the gift. Included in them are prohibitions against a man having sexual relations with: his mother, his father's wife, his sister, his son's daughter, his aunt, his daughter-in-law, a woman and her daughter, his wife's sister while his wife is still alive, his sister-in-law, his neighbor's wife, or with a woman who is menstruating (Leviticus 18). Omitted from the list, oddly enough, is a prohibition against a man having sexual relations with his daughter. There are numerous caveats that accompany some of these prohibitions. For instance, if a woman's husband dies before she has a son, it is the duty of her husband's brother to marry her (Deuteronomy 25). If a man has sex with an engaged woman in the city, they are both to be executed, but if the sex occurs in the countryside (where no one can hear her scream), then only he is to be stoned (Deuteronomy 22). As with most attempts at regulation, these laws (and the many others) fall short. Essentially, they assert that as long as a man doesn't have sex with a family member, another man's wife, another man, or an animal, then sex is acceptable. But, adherence to these rules does not guarantee healthy, safe sex. Some of the most heinous acts imaginable are perpetrated within the limits of these laws. Human sexuality is much too complex and too precious a gift to be defined by some list of rules.

Misogyny, Idolatry, and Nationalism

Defining a clear sexual ethic in scripture is extremely challenging because sexuality is hopelessly entangled with misogyny (prejudice against women), idolatry (worship of false gods), and nationalism. Beyond the most basic of prohibitions listed above, it's difficult to ascertain if certain sexual activity is inherently bad or if it's bad due to its association with another issue. For instance, is premarital sex a sin in and of itself, or does the Bible treat it as sinful because it would prevent the girl's father from receiving a dowry (misogyny)? Or again, is homosexuality sinful because of the act itself or because it doesn't produce soldiers for Israel's army (nationalism)?

Take, for example, the story of Onan and Tamar in Genesis 38. Tamar's husband died before she had a son. In accordance with the law listed above, her husband's brother Onan was responsible to "Sleep with [his] brother's wife and fulfill [his] duty to her as a brother-in-law to raise up offspring for [his] brother" (Genesis 38:8). Onan objected to the law and rebelled by withdrawing and spilling his semen on the ground. For this act, God punished him with death! But, what was the real sin? Many have used the passage to denounce masturbation arguing that Onan was killed for spilling his semen. That argument denies the fact that Onan was having sex with a woman, not masturbating. Perhaps, Onan sinned against his country. The promise God made to Abraham was that God would turn Abraham and Sarah's family into a great nation. Part of Israel's sexual morality is predicated on this promise. Going from one family to a great nation requires making lots of babies. Sexual acts like spilling seed, and homosexuality violate that nationalistic cause. Birth control would have been viewed just as negatively. Misogyny is also a factor in Onan's story. In ancient Israel, Tamar was property with no legal rights of her own. Without a son or a father, her likely options for survival were begging or prostitution. Because of the culture, Onan was condemning Tamar to a difficult life. In that case, the sin was not sexual, but cultural (devaluing women).

The impact of misogyny is even more obvious

when considering the following law. "If a man happens to meet a virgin who is not pledged to be married and rapes her and they are discovered, he shall pay her father fifty shekels of silver. He must marry the young woman, for he has violated her. He can never divorce her as long as he lives" (Deuteronomy 22:28-29 NIV). Notice, first, that this law refers to a woman who is not engaged. Were she engaged, the punishment for intercourse would be death. Because she is not engaged, she is still the property of her father. In ancient times, sons were considered an economic asset and daughters an economic liability. The father of a daughter expected some compensation in the form of a dowry, but only if she is still a virgin when she marries. Girls who were not virgins were not likely candidates for marriage at all. The man in question, has essentially taken a wife without paying for her, thus the fine of 50 shekels. This man must also assume lifelong responsibility for the woman. He must meet all of her basic needs for food, clothing and shelter, because the loss of her virginity meant that she would not likely find a decent husband. To be fair, not all translations agree whether the sex in this verse is rape or consensual. In either case, though, neither pre-marital sex nor sexual assault is condemned as sinful in and of themselves. The sin is actually not sexual at all but theft of property.

The situation for women doesn't improve much in the New Testament. In John 8, religious leaders try to trap Jesus by confronting him with a woman caught in the act of adultery. They remind Jesus that Moses commanded that adulterers be stoned. They asked his opinion. If Jesus said to stone her, he opposed his own teaching of love and forgiveness. If he forgave her, he violated the law of Moses. His famous response to the accusers—"Let any one of you who is without sin be the first to throw a stone at her" (John 8:7b NIV). Of course, everyone walked away, and Jesus forgave the woman. The question in the story that never gets asked is, "Where was the man?" The law commanded that both guilty parties be stoned. The male religious leaders ignored the full law and used a "disposable" woman as a prop in their evil plan. These are just three examples of the difficulty of developing a solid Biblical sexual ethic because of cultural differences in the value of women.

The intermingling of idolatry with sexuality only serves to complicate matters further. One of the most common false religions during Old Testament times was the worship of fertility gods. The temptation should not be surprising. Survival depended on good crops and strong reproduction of livestock. The unpredictability of both led to superstition which led to cult practices. The "doctrine" of fertility religions is quite simple. Seasonally, a male god impregnates mother earth and causes her to spring forth with new crops. In that belief system, the role of worship is to sexually stimulate the god into action. Worship included men from the village going down to the local temple to have sex with prostitutes in an effort to arouse the fertility god. (Talk about a religion designed by men for men.) Worship of fertility gods is one of Israel's most consistent sins in the Old Testament and the subject of the book of Hosea.

The Bible does tell us to abstain from sexual immorality (1 Thessalonians 4:3), but it doesn't offer a clear definition. Which sexual acts are inherently immoral, and which are immoral only because of their connection to idolatry or misogyny? Some objectionable sexual behavior is actually allowed in the Bible. In Old Testament times, a man could claim any unattached woman he wanted even if he already had one or more wives. Typically, the women had no choice in the matter. The modern church abhors both forced marriage and polygamy, even though they are solidly Biblical. We will continue to pursue a positive sexual ethic in this chapter, but first let's turn our attention to a related issue—modesty.

Modesty—If You're Female

Paul's instruction to women to dress modestly and discreetly has been wielded like a weapon against women for centuries. I taught in a Christian school where the straps on all girl's dresses had to be three fingers wide and the hem four fingers below the knee. I've been a part of youth ministries that insisted on one-piece bathing suits for girls. The onus always seems to be on the girl to keep it decent. I heard parents tell a story of their poor, oppressed son. We'll call him Joe. Like good Christians, they taught Joe not to look at females in immodest clothing. Their instruction to him when in the presence of such women was to "avert the eyes." One summer afternoon, that young family attended a church picnic. Many of the young women present wore sun dresses. The exposure to so much skin caused Joe to rush to his parents in a panic. "I don't know where to look," he said, "there's nowhere to avert the eyes." Joe's mom told the story as part of a plea to Christian women to dress more modestly. First, in my opinion, sun dresses are not immodest. Second, and more important, our culture places undue responsibility on women for men's behavior, and it's an insult to both. Perhaps the parents would have done better to help Joe make mature responses to visual stimuli.

Current Christian views on modesty assume that men can't control sexual urges, so women are responsible for making them behave. In the worst cases, we blame victims of rape for "asking for it" because of the way they were dressed. Our efforts to be holy in our attire are actually causing harm as this woman attests in an article in Christianity Today (October 2013).

I was told that being a Christian woman meant protecting men's minds by the way that I dressed. That's what Jesus wanted. So, I lugged a trash bag full of short skirts, dresses, cropped shirts, and tube tops out to the dumpster—determined to dress modestly and respect my body as a temple of the Holy Spirit. Take up your cross and follow, right? I replaced my midriff baring shirts with hoodies. I moved to China to share the gospel, where I stopped wearing makeup and didn't care much about my style. But like many Christian women, I found that dressing modestly wasn't the answer to all my problems. It didn't stop me from "causing" men to lust or stumble. (So said the people who once again reminded me to "be careful" about how I dressed). And this forced modesty didn't make me feel any better about myself. I didn't feel beautiful or confident wearing loose T-shirts and gaining weight. Covering up made me feel worthless, just as trying to dress "sexy" had made me feel unworthy. Both approaches establish our view of ourselves and our bodies according to a man's response, rather than allowing us to recognize our inherent value and beauty as women of God. Whether we see our body as a beautiful object that men desire or one that is dirty and needs to be covered up—we're still living in fear. And fear is contrary to the gospel.

Fear of the human body is definitely contrary to the image of the kingdom revealed in the Garden of Eden.

I often remind people that the only time the world was perfect everybody was naked. Of course, I'm not arguing that the world should become one big nudist colony. I'm just trying to illustrate that our fear of the human body is unhealthy. Recently, while watching a television drama in prime time on a broadcast network, I saw a woman's head blown off her body in graphic detail. Blood and grey matter spattered the sidewalk and pedestrians. This violence is widely acceptable entertainment in our culture. However, had the same woman exposed a nipple, the show would have been censored and would have drawn at least a PG-13 rating from the MPAA. Even a mother breast-feeding in public creates more outrage than the violence we allow in our living rooms nightly under the guise of entertainment. How did we get to a place as a society where seeing a nipple is more offensive than a beheading?

If we dare, we may discover that nudity can actually be healing as revealed in another article from Christianity Today (June 6, 2014).

And then I read Zanthe Taylor's piece, "The Glories of Nudity," detailing her experience at a Korean spa in which mothers and daughters bathe naked alongside dozens of other nude women. As Taylor writes, "It was challenging to disrobe without feeling utterly exposed, but I didn't want to show my daughter I was fazed by it, so I stripped off and closed the locker door on my clothes." Her essay goes on to describe the freedom she felt in this experience, which was not in any way sexual in nature but rather an opportunity to see herself and other women without being ashamed of her body. She also describes the astonishing array of bodies all around her and how different it is to form a view of women's bodies from real women rather than magazine cover models. She never uses the word shame, and yet I was struck by how much the experience could help her form—for herself and her daughters—a positive understanding of her body as a good gift rather than a necessary but corrupted vessel.

Naked and unashamed, that's the way the author of Genesis describes our first parents. Modesty rules run the risk of encouraging people, especially females, to despise the gift God gave us in our bodies.

Still, some will argue, "Paul told women to dress discreetly. We're just following the Bible." Let's look a little more closely at that passage. "Likewise, I want women to adorn themselves with proper clothing, modestly and discreetly, not with braided hair and gold or pearls or costly garments, but rather by means of good works, as is proper for women making a claim to godliness" (1 Timothy 2:9-10). First, notice what Paul does not say. There is no mention of dress length or cleavage, no guidelines on how much skin can show. What Paul does discourage is expensive clothing. It's immodest, says Paul, to show up for worship in expensive clothing when some of the other people present don't have enough to eat. It's immodest to flaunt wealth in the presence of poverty. The modern church in America won't hesitate to attack women for the length of their dresses, but it's not about to challenge the display of wealth. Maybe our modesty rules are not designed to produce holiness. Perhaps their intent is to control women and exonerate men for bad behavior.

Homosexuality

If modest clothing for women is one of the church's favorite targets, homosexuality is another. Early in my career as a pastor I discovered the attraction of attacking homosexuals. As the Pharisees before me used women as a prop to trap Jesus, I used homosexuals as a prop to win the acclaim of my heterosexual church membership. Every good cause needs a villain. Unfortunately, I villainized homosexuals. Sadly, I said hateful things from the pulpit, in the name of Jesus, and earned a pat on the back from worshippers and the acclamation, "Way to be tough on sin, preacher!" In the 1980s, homosexuals were an easy target. If there were any in my churches, they were not out, and preaching against that lifestyle was safer than attacking sins that I knew all of us committed, like greed, gossip, and failure to love our enemies. Having a convenient villain allowed us to live with the illusion that we were the good guys, God's chosen, because we weren't a part of that lifestyle.

A weeklong family camping trip put the first crack in my world view. After pitching our tent, we discovered that our next-door neighbors were a lesbian couple camping with their son. These women were no villains. They were delightful. They were loving, of each other and of us. Because they were in a camper, they had better resources than we had with our tent. They shared freely. After preaching against homosexuals for years, this week provided my first known encounter with some of the people I villainized. I'm not sure what I expected. What I discovered was people who acted more like Jesus than a lot of church people. My encounter with this wonderful couple led me back to the scriptures. Exactly what do they have to say about homosexuality?

The "go to" text for many who oppose homosexuality is the story of the destruction of Sodom and Gomorrah. In the story, God sends male angels to the cities to destroy them. While the angels are the guests of Abraham's nephew Lot, the men of the city come and demand the opportunity to forcefully have sex with the visitors. Lot doesn't allow it, and God destroys the city for its sin. Rather than an indictment of homosexuality, the sin that is exposed is rape. The men of the city wanted to assault the angels. Ezekiel clarifies the sin of Sodom further. "Now this was the sin of your sister Sodom: She and her daughters were arrogant, overfed and unconcerned; they did not help the poor and needy. They were haughty and did detestable things before me. Therefore, I did away with them as you have seen" (Ezekiel 16:49-50 NIV). If homosexuality was the great sin of Sodom, Ezekiel missed the memo! He was more concerned with greed.

Leviticus does prohibit a man from laying with a

man as he lays with a woman. For many, that commandment is proof enough. The punishment for breaking that law, though, is that they shall both be put to death (Leviticus 20:13). Many people in our culture oppose homosexuality. No sane person is calling for the execution of homosexuals. Yet, it is hard to claim one half of a verse as authoritative while dismissing the other half of the verse.

The New Testament offers the favorite "clobber passages" for those who oppose homosexuality, Romans 1:26-28, and I Corinthians 6:9-11. The latter claims that homosexuals will not inherit the kingdom of God. While there were multiple words in Greek for homosexual activity, Paul chose to coin a new word for the Corinthians, *arsenokoitai*. Scholars continue to debate the meaning, and it's beyond the scope of this book to explore all the possibilities in depth. Explanations range from homosexual behavior to forced sex between a man and a boy to temple prostitution. As the following sample illustrates, English translations of the Bible struggle to provide a clear definition of *arsenokoitai*.

King James	Effeminate, abusers of themselves with mankind
New International	Men who have sex with men
American Standard	Effeminate, abusers of themselves with men
Contemporary English	Behaves like a homosexual
English Standard	Men who practice homosexuality
Geneva Study Bible	Buggerers
The Message	Use and abuse sex

New Revised Standard	Male prostitutes, sodomites
Revised Standard	Sexual perverts

If Paul was referring specifically to homosexual relationships, then why not use one of the words that would provide clarity? Even if we accept the modern idea of homosexuality as the definition of the Greek word, we are still left with a couple of dilemmas. The alleged prohibition against homosexuality comes at the end of a much more severe indictment of Christians who sue one another. "The very fact that you have lawsuits among you means you have been completely defeated already. Why not rather be wronged? Why not rather be cheated?" (I Corinthians 6:7). This same Corinthian text that criticizes lawsuits also excludes the greedy from the kingdom of heaven. While much has been said of purifying the church of homosexuality, no one wants to address our greed. We clergy judge ourselves by the size of our salaries, our churches, our staffs, and our homes. Greed is our measuring stick. Some argue that we are repentant of our greed, but we're not. If we were repentant, we would give away our stuff and follow Jesus. A church that ordains the greedy and the litigious is acting out of hypocrisy when it excludes homosexuals.

Romans chapter one appears to make the point that homosexual acts are shameful, but upon further examination we discover that the real sin is in verses 22-23. "Although they claimed to be wise, they became fools and exchanged the glory of the immortal God for images made to look like a mortal human being and birds and animals and reptiles." The sin for which the Romans faced judgement was worshipping the creature rather than the Creator—

idolatry. In the list of things that follow in Romans 1, homosexual acts are equated with disobedience to parents, hardly the kind of thing that exempts one from service in the kingdom. As we've seen with the rest of our discussion of sexuality, it is nearly impossible to disentangle sexual morality from idolatry and misogyny.

Known By Our Fruits

There must be a better way. Those opposing homosexuality remind us that we must be faithful to scripture, that the Bible is our authority for Christian living. So, maybe the Bible does offer some clarity. In the Sermon on the Mount, Jesus said, "By their fruit you will recognize them. Do people pick grapes from thorn bushes, or figs from thistles? Likewise, every good tree bears good fruit, but a bad tree bears bad fruit. A good tree cannot bear bad fruit, and a bad tree cannot bear good fruit. Every tree that does not bear good fruit is cut down and thrown into the fire. Thus, by their fruit you will recognize them" (Matthew 7:16-20 NIV). I know homosexuals in ministry who have led thousands of people to Christ. Their lives exhibit love, joy, peace, patience, goodness, kindness, faithfulness, gentleness, and self-control. If these people were "bad trees," they could not bear such fruit, if Jesus is right. The evidence of their discipleship is not who they sleep with but what fruit they produce! Imagine what more they could do if we didn't judge them as bad trees!

Ultimately, God will judge me for my beliefs and actions, and I may be wrong. But, I would rather be found guilty of welcoming too many than too few.

On the Horizon

Despite a lack of Biblical clarity, Christian denominations, including my own, continue to split over beliefs about homosexuality. Our tardiness to the conversation makes the church even more irrelevant to our culture. For the majority of Americans, the issue is resolved, and public discussion is moving to other issues. The church is already behind in the discussion of transsexuals and is oblivious to polyamory, which is already visible on the cultural horizon. Different from "swinging," which focuses on open sexual experiences, polyamory, literally "many loves," is a term that includes intimate, committed relationships between three or more people. It also differs from the more paternalistic polygamous relationships that feature one man with multiple wives. Polyamorous relationships tend to be more maternalistic and occur in various combinations of men and women. Unless it learns to have honest, loving, grace-filled conversations about human sexuality, a church that is still sharply divided over homosexuality will be ill-equipped to offer Good News in the sexual landscape of the not-too-distant future.

A Difficult Topic

Human sexuality is a difficult topic, one that many in the church would rather ignore. If you're one of those, you're not alone. It may seem that life would be easier if we could just ignore sex. St. Augustine, one of the greatest teachers in the history of the church, condemned sexual pleasure for everyone. Although, among spouses he considered such pleasure to be only a venial sin. England banned the

Oscar Wilde play Salome' about the beheading of John the Baptist claiming it was "half Biblical, half pornographic." I suppose the British could only endure a polite beheading of a prophet. It's amazing to think that sexuality is the evil part of that story! Even into the early 1900s, sex for reasons other than procreation was considered taboo.

While the topic is difficult, I dare address it because the Bible does. Pure, perfect sexuality is present in the creation story. Protagonists confront their sexuality throughout multiple stories in the scriptures. And, an entire book is devoted to celebrating sexual intimacy. If we will be honest with ourselves, Song of Solomon is nothing short of an erotic poem. Sadly, translators who were also apparently fearful of sexuality, cleaned up portions of it. But, listen, if your dare, to the original meaning of its text. Preston Sprinkle tells the story of a visiting professor teaching his Bible class on the Song of Solomon.

> I'll never forget feeling the tension in the classroom as he went into detail about the real meaning of the poem. "His body is polished ivory," says the ESV, but according to Tremper, the Hebrew word for body refers to the man's midsection and the image of ivory is intended to invoke the original form of ivory: an elephant's tusk. Yes, that's right. The wife in Song of Songs 5:14 is admiring her well-hung husband.

That Bible study will get a pastor thrown out of a lot of churches. And, that's sad, because our sexuality if a gift from God.

Sex as Grace

Former Archbishop of Canterbury Rowan Williams suggests that healthy sex is an expression of grace. In the church, we talk about grace; we sing about grace; we develop complex theories about grace; but we have few ways to tangibly experience it. Grace is that unearned gift of pure unconditional love that God gives. On our worst day, God loves us. That love is a miracle, one that can manifest itself in a healthy sexual relationship. Partners come together, naked, exposed, vulnerable. On display are wrinkles, moles and fat rolls. They would be horrified if the scene were ever made public. But, in private they find acceptance and love in a partner's embrace. Love that doesn't see imperfections, that offers itself freely, and seeks the pleasure of the other—these are acts of grace that give us hope that God truly does love who we really are. Healthy sex is not defined by some long list of ancient rules. Rather it is defined by partners giving their best to each other and eliciting the very best from each other. It's loving, affirming, and cherishing. It seeks to honor the other. Holy, healthy sex is proof that we are lovable.

4 DUCK, LUCK, AND OTHER RHYMING WORDS

Sticks and stones may break my bones,
But words will never hurt me.

I learned the rhyme as a young child. I also learned as a young child that these words are a lie. Words can hurt! They hurt me over and over for years. Around the time I was in second grade, classmates started discovering all the things that were wrong with me: crooked teeth, snotty nose, and worst of all a big head. To their delight, those same classmates also discovered that they could make me cry. Bullies prey on weakness, and my tears made me appear weak. Elementary school kids can be cruel. I walked down school hallways to the chants of "Tank Head," and I could feel the tears well up inside me. I knew they were just words. My physical attributes were out of my control, and my family still loved me. In spite of those reassurances, I battled those tears to avoid the next chants of "Cry Baby." It's a battle I usually lost. I suffered the blows of those words each time they were spoken well into my junior high years. And, they hurt each time I heard them. None of the words was profanity, by our usual definition. It wasn't a "four-letter word" that stabbed into my soul, but ordinary, acceptable words used in hateful ways. I had nowhere to turn. Our teachers would have punished profanity, but teasing was just what little boys did, and nobody considered it profane.

During those same years, I became aware of profanity, or cussing as we called it, but I never equated it with the hateful things said to me by my classmates. On the contrary, cuss words made me feel good. They were forbidden, and they tasted good rolling off my tongue. Unlike the "acceptable" words that stung so badly, "four-letter" words empowered me. They granted me the illusion that I was one of the tough, cool kids. Cry-babies don't cuss, so I found comfort in a foul mouth, though never within earshot of an adult. Parents and teachers tended to have really negative reactions to such colorful language, but I never really understood why. Unlike "Tank Head," these words didn't hurt me. Mostly, they were slang words for body parts or bodily functions. It didn't make sense that a different initial consonant would make the words luck or duck deplorable. I didn't know why those words were evil, but I did know not to speak them in front of adults, or punishment would follow.

Cleaning Up My Language

During my junior high years, I became convinced of the evils of profanity. In the summer after my eighth-grade year, I had a profound spiritual experience that would shape the rest of my life. While I already believed in God, I made a commitment to follow Christ more closely. Part of that commitment was to abstain from profanity, to clean up my language. Still not sure of why "four letter words" were wrong, I resolved to ban them from my language at precisely the time that I started playing football. The irony of that timing may be lost on any that never played football, but foul language is the language of the sport. The weight room and the practice field were consistently R-rated. Huddles were obscene, especially when we were losing, which was often. At half-time, the coach could release a string of words at 15-year-olds that would make a sailor blush. Still, I kept my commitment. I didn't join in their vile language, and I was proud of myself for it. To be honest, I enjoyed my spiritual superiority and was sure that God was impressed as well. Every day, I walked away from the locker room feeling grateful that I wasn't like those other guys with gutter mouths. In my fervor to be holy, I became a Pharisee, and I never saw it coming.

My self-righteous year in football illustrates, again, the fallacy of morality. Because I followed a cultural, moral code regarding language, I assumed that God was pleased with me, actually more pleased with me than with my foul-mouthed teammates. Because of their language, they deserved God's wrath and my contempt. I was okay. They weren't. And, it was all because of language. I acted as though I didn't need grace, and as though they weren't good enough for it.

Evolution of Profanity

Surely, there's more to Christianity than abstaining from profanity, especially when our "cuss words" didn't even exist in Biblical times. In fact, the English language didn't exist. While serving my first church, I developed a friendship with a wonderful couple who we'll call Bill and Susan. They were in their eighties and were big supporters of their young preacher, and I treasure them for that encouragement. During one of my visits at their house, Bill declared that he knew what was wrong with the church. I was anxious to hear his answer but managed to contain my shock when he said, "They got away from the King James Bible. It was good enough for Jesus. It ought to be good enough for us." Susan just rolled her eyes. It was useless to try to convince Bill that the Bible was written in Hebrew and Greek and that nobody spoke English during the days that Jesus walked the planet. While most modern people don't share Bill's worldview, cultural Christianity does act as though Jesus provided a list of words in English that faithful Christians should never say out loud, or even think. Such a list does not exist. Still, in an attempt to be Christian, we enforce our arbitrary standards. My son discovered that truth while attending a Christian high school. While on a field trip, he told a classmate to shut the hell up. For his verbal transgression, the head football coach paddled him, even though profanity was the language of football at his Christian school, too. What irony!

Not only did English not exist in Biblical times, our language continues to evolve. What is acceptable in one time period may be taboo in the next. Racial slurs change over time. As I child, I remember TV commercials soliciting support for the United Negro College Fund. Surely, a fund supporting majority African-American schools was not using Negro as a pejorative, but today, the same word is insulting to many people. Our language, including profanity, changes. When I studied psychology in college, the text books taught me that anyone with an IQ of 70 or below was retarded. Once a scientific, diagnostic word, that word is now offensive. Even if the church could formulate a Biblically based list of profane words, the list would be obsolete within a decade.

The Power of Words

I don't mean to imply that our words are not important. The book of James in the Bible cautions us about the use of the tongue. "The tongue also is a fire, a world of evil among the parts of the body. It corrupts the whole body, sets the whole course of one's life on fire, and is itself set on fire by hell" (James 3:6). But, what makes the tongue so dangerous? Cuss words? Or, is more implied in this verse. In Ephesians 5:4, Paul discourages obscenity and coarse joking and suggest instead that we use our words for thanksgiving. But, Paul is also willing to use obscenity when he feels it's appropriate for emphasis. In Philippians 3:8, Paul explains that all his former accomplishments are *skubala* when compared with the greatness of knowing Christ. *Skubala* is a Greek word that is often translated as garbage or dung by English translators fearful of offending our delicate sensibilities. A more accurate translation would be crap or shit. This verse is the only time the word appears in the Bible, so it's probably inaccurate to accuse the Apostles of being foul-mouthed. However, this verse does illustrate Paul's willingness to cuss to make a point. There are other examples where the translators felt obligated to clean up the language of the original text. When Elijah battled the prophets of Ba'al on Mt. Carmel, he accused their god of having "gone aside" or in modern terms, gone to pee (I Kings 18:27 NASB). In Daniel 5, King Belshazzar's loins are loosed. He craps his pants. And, the Song of Solomon in the original language is far too explicit for the ears of the modern moral Christian. My parents often told me the story of how the movie Gone with the Wind was considered scandalous for the use of the word damn. By the same standard, the Bible would have been banned from school reading lists for its obscenity.

The Bible does clearly condemn taking the Lord's name in vain. We commonly interpret that commandment to be a prohibition against connecting the word god to the "four-letter word," damn, and we are correct to do so, but the commandment extends much further. The commandment also prohibits any careless use of God's name or of using God's name to support one's own position. When our politicians invoke God's name in support for their own campaigns or platforms, unless God fully supports their position, they are taking God's name in vain. In this case, it's not a particular word that defines profanity but using our words to misrepresent or disrespect a God who loves us unconditionally.

True Profanity

So, words are important and can cause injury, but our culture's obsessions with certain words we call profane may be misguided. How do we sort out the truth? How will we define profanity? Tony Campolo offers a helpful illustration.

I have three things I'd like to say today. First, while you were sleeping last night, 30,000 kids died of starvation or diseases related to malnutrition. Second, most of you don't give a shit. What's worse is that you're more upset with the fact that I

said shit than the fact that 30,000 kids died last
night.

Campolo astutely reveals our problem with profanity.
We mistakenly define profanity in terms of words, not
people. Children starving to death in a world that
produces plenty of food is profane!

My friend Terry lived in a broken-down trailer
about half a mile behind our church. My wife and I
met Terry in the middle of a cold winter. There were
holes in the walls and the floor of his home. His
primary source of heat was a wood burning stove
haphazardly vented through his living room window.
After nearly burning down his trailer, he stopped
using the stove and relied on an electric space heater
instead. On cold nights, he and his dogs would sleep
under as many blankets as he could find. Next to his
bed was a mason jar that he used as a chamber pot,
because it was too cold to go outside to use the
bathroom, and there was no indoor plumbing. Terry
described to me his process for taking a bath. He
would go out to his well to get water which he would
heat on his stove and pour into a five-gallon bucket.
He placed a piece of plywood over the bucket to hold
the heat while he retrieved and heated a second pot of
water. After adding it to the bucket, he bathed with
the water from that five-gallon bucket. People who
were used to the conveniences of tubs and showers
criticized him for being dirty. "Soap and water are
cheap," they said. But, they didn't take the time to
learn the difficulties Terry faced with routine hygiene.
At least once, he tried to attend the church I served. I
learned, later, that he was turned away because he
wasn't dressed appropriately for church. It's hard to
dress to impress when you live like Terry, and he

shouldn't have had to impress anyone to come to church. He left and never returned. So, we invited Terry to our small group. We shared meals together, laughed together and became friends. Our small group adopted Terry, not as a project but as a friend. He wanted the opportunity to get a shower and a haircut, so we made it happen. One night as my wife and I drove him home from dinner with our group, Terry told us again and again, "Tonight has been the best night of my life." Unconditional love has that effect. The next June I was assigned to a new church. Our small group dissolved and, with it, Terry's only connection to the church. On December 11, 2017, Terry froze to death within the shadow of a church that I used to serve. If I dropped the "f-bomb" in a Sunday morning sermon, there would be phone calls to my superiors, and committee meetings, and disciplinary actions, and perhaps there should be. But, it's not the "f-bomb" that's profane. It's Terry's death! It's pure profanity that a human being would freeze to death while an empty church remains heated enough to protect the pipes from bursting! Too often we value our buildings over our people, and that's profane!

Of course, words can be profane, too, but not because they rhyme with duck or because they are slang for body parts and bodily functions. Words are profane when they insult God or demean and dehumanize people. When my classmates chanted "Tank Head," those words were profanity. When we direct words like idiot, dummy, or fatso at fellow humans, we are speaking profanity. Shouting an expletive when you slam your finger in a door does no real damage. Calling someone worthless does. In the Sermon on the Mount, Jesus said that the person who calls another a fool will be in danger of hell fire, because words that dehumanize are profanity!

5 A GLUTTON AND A DRUNKARD

"A Difference in Beliefs"
The Jews don't recognize Jesus as the Messiah.
Protestants don't recognize the Pope as the head of the
church.
Baptists don't recognize one another in the liquor store.

I first heard the joke decades ago, and it stuck with me, because it's funny, and because there's some truth in it. While I didn't grow up in the Baptist church, I certainly identify with the final line of the joke. There was never alcohol in my parent's house. During our daily morning devotions, I often heard my parents praying that my oldest brother and his wife would stop drinking alcohol. I still recall all the drama that occurred the night my teenage brother came home from a party drunk. He later made me promise never to drink alcohol, even though he continued drinking. By the time I was a teenager, I seriously doubted whether someone who drinks alcohol, even socially, could be a real Christian. My church youth group shared my opinion, and together, we abstained from alcohol and criticized anyone who dared to drink. Our temperance filled us with an air of superiority. As far as we were concerned, alcohol was evil, and there was no disputing it.

We were not alone. Much of cultural Christianity continues to hold the view that real Christians don't drink. One night at a dinner party, the host pulled me aside to ask if I would mind saying a blessing over the meal. He was concerned I might be offended because there was alcohol on the table. I told him I would be happy to say the blessing, but I found it odd that he thought the presence of cocktails was a reason not to pray. His concern highlights the taboo of drinking among much of the church culture. In 2006, the Southern Baptist Convention passed the following resolution that leaves little doubt about their opinion of the dangers of drinking.

WHEREAS, Years of research confirm biblical warnings that alcohol use leads to physical, mental, and emotional damage (e.g., Proverbs 23:29-35); and

WHEREAS, Alcohol use has led to countless injuries and deaths on our nation's highways; and

WHEREAS, The breakup of families and homes can be directly and indirectly attributed to alcohol use by one or more members of a family; and

WHEREAS, The use of alcohol as a recreational beverage has been shown to lead individuals down a path of addiction to alcohol and toward the use of other kinds of drugs, both legal and illegal; and

WHEREAS, There are some religious leaders who are now advocating the consumption of alcoholic beverages based on a misinterpretation of the doctrine of "our freedom in Christ"; now, therefore, be it

RESOLVED, That the messengers to the Southern Baptist Convention meeting in Greensboro, North Carolina, June 13-14, 2006, express our total opposition to the manufacturing, advertising, distributing, and consuming of alcoholic beverages; and be it further

RESOLVED, That we urge that no one be elected to serve as a trustee or member of any entity or committee of the Southern Baptist Convention that is a user of alcoholic beverages.

RESOLVED, That we urge Southern Baptists to take an active role in supporting legislation that is intended to curb alcohol use in our communities and nation; and be it further

RESOLVED, That we urge Southern Baptists to be actively involved in educating students and adults concerning the destructive nature of alcoholic beverages; and be it finally

RESOLVED, That we commend organizations and ministries that treat alcohol-related problems from a biblical perspective and promote abstinence and encourage local churches to begin and/or support such biblically-based ministries.

An entire denomination of church goers expresses their "total opposition to the manufacturing, advertising, distributing, and consuming of alcoholic beverages!" Pastor Barney Lee of West Seneca, New

York adds his opinion, "In fact, if the preacher is to stick to his Bible, preach the whole truth, and be fair to the Word of God, he MUST preach against alcohol." Apparently, it's witch's brew, and the devil himself is the bartender. As with other types of morality, those who completely follow the rules assume that they must be inside the faith family, and those who break the rules must be outside. If the moral code is firmly rooted in scripture, if it honors the teachings of Christ and the Apostles, then abstinence is a bold, prophetic stand. If, however, the scriptures do not demand abstinence, then those who do may be adding unnecessary burdens to salvation. As Christians, the teaching of Jesus should guide our behavior rather than the resolutions of a religious body.

The Bible and Alcohol

So, what does the Bible say about alcohol? A lot, actually, and it includes celebrations of strong drink as well as cautions. The Bible mentions wine approximately 230 times and beer nine times, depending on the translation, but the message varies. Those individuals who took a vow as a Nazarite, like Samson, completely abstained from alcohol, but that requirement is strictly for those who take the vow. In Psalm 104, wine is a gift from God, "He makes grass grow for the cattle, and plants for people to cultivate—bringing forth food from the earth: wine that gladdens human hearts, oil to make their faces shine, and bread that sustains their hearts" (14-15). Proverbs 20:1 counters, "Wine is a mocker and beer a brawler; whoever is led astray by them is not wise," but the same book suggests that wine is a reward from God for faithfulness. "Honor the Lord with your wealth, with the firstfruits of all your crops; then your barns will be filled to overflowing and your vats will brim over with new wine" (3:9-10). In the New Testament, Paul cautions, "Do not get drunk on wine, which leads to debauchery. Instead, be filled with the Spirit" (Ephesians 5:18). But, Jesus affirms that He "came eating and drinking," and the people called Him "a glutton and a drunkard" (Matthew 11:19). The contrasting themes are consistent throughout the scriptures. There are dozens of cautions against drunkenness but also many affirmations of wine used in celebrations, the most notable of which was Jesus' miracle at the wedding in Cana of Galilee. The story is in the second chapter of the Gospel of John. The wedding guests drank all the wine that the family provided and were still wanting more. At the request of His mother, Jesus transformed six pots of water into wine totaling approximately 150 gallons! After the guests had drunk freely, He made that much more wine! Some have argued that wine in the New Testament was not alcoholic or that it was less alcoholic. That argument has little merit due to the numerous prohibitions against getting drunk with wine. As uncomfortable as it is for some, the fact remains that when the crowd had already celebrated liberally, Jesus added a lot more wine to keep the party going. The Bible offers a clear argument for caution regarding alcohol but no prohibition against it.

Church History and Alcohol

Not only does the Bible fail to condemn the consumptions of alcohol, neither does most of church history. Medieval monasteries actually produced beer and wine, often inventing new techniques to improve their product. In 1620, the ship that brought John Winthrop to the Massachusetts Bay Colony also transported 10,000 gallons of wine (Conlin 43). Even the Puritans of the American northeast didn't ban alcohol. In 1673, Increase Mather published *Wo to Drunkards* which affirms, "Drink is in itself a good creature of God, and to be received with thankfulness, but the abuse of drink is from Satan, the wine is from God, but the Drunkard is from the Devil" (Harris).

Temperance

It wasn't until 1805 that Rev. Ebenezer Porter preached America's first temperance sermon, "The Fatal Effects of Ardent Spirits" (Porter). During the 1800s, abuse of alcohol led to numerous problems throughout the American culture including absenteeism at work, job loss, divorce, and physical abuse toward wives and children. Such evils led to the temperance movement which quickly became enmeshed with the Christian church. In fact, most major American denominations that oppose alcohol consumption were founded during the 19th and early 20th centuries, during the temperance movement.

Churches that Oppose Alcohol Consumption

Denomination	Date Founded
Southern Baptist	1845
Church of Christ	Early 1800s
Church of the Nazarene	1908
Salvation Army	1865
Assembly of God	1914
Church of God	1922

The predominant social cause of the time period became a part of the founding DNA of the institutions.

In 1869, a Methodist pastor developed a technique for pasteurizing grape juice, a product he quickly marketed throughout the denomination for use in its communion services. The pastor's name—Rev. Thomas Welch of Welch's Grape Juice fame.

The Women's Christian Temperance Union formed in 1874, and the temperance movement united with the church in a nationwide effort to abolish alcohol, a goal which they partially achieved with the ratification of the 18th Amendment to the United States Constitution which states, "After one year from the ratification of this article, the manufacture sale, or transportation of intoxicating liquors within, the importation thereof into, or the exportation thereof from the Unites States and all territory subject to the jurisdictions thereof for beverage purposes is hereby prohibited." The amendment took effect on January 17, 1920, but the production, distribution, and sales of alcohol continued through homemade distilleries (stills), bootleggers, and speakeasies. In 1933, the 18th Amendment became the only amendment to the U. S. Constitution to be repealed, thus ending 13 years of Prohibition. The effects continue to linger, though. Numerous counties, especially in the South, remain dry, and in many states where alcohol is sold, the tax from its sales is officially referred to as "sin tax." The overwhelming evidence from Biblical and church history strongly suggests that any prohibition against consuming alcohol is rooted in the socio/political history of the last two hundred years, not the teaching of Christ or the Apostles. If the church makes abstaining from alcohol a condition for salvation, baptism, or church membership, it is requiring more than Christ requires.

Alcohol and Morality

Some churches concede that their stance against alcohol is not Biblically based, but they argue that the evils listed above are more than enough reason to require abstinence. In fighting what they believe is a good cause, I'm afraid they are shutting the door of the kingdom of Heaven to many people, people like Brad. Brad was an active member in one of my churches. He and his family rarely missed worship. He and his wife served in church leadership, and the children were active in our children's ministry. Brad enjoyed an ice-cold beer at the end of his long workday, and he made it clear that he wouldn't be attending any church that told him he couldn't. Some might accuse him of making his beer more important than church. I suspect many churches make their rules more important than people. There is no Biblical basis for turning Brad away from church. The church has no business being pickier than God!

The church is blatantly hypocritical when it attempts to prohibit alcohol consumption because of the dangers it poses. According to the Center for Disease Control, there are 88,000 alcohol related deaths per year in the United States. Those are tragic deaths, and that number, alone, supports a strong case for moderation. Obesity, however, kills 300,000 people per year and is the second leading cause of preventable death in the United States. Very few churches dare to serve alcohol, but every church I've served is proud of its covered dish luncheons where tables are weighed down with fried chicken, pork roasts, macaroni and cheese, and banana pudding. The cooks who prepare these feasts line the hallways, eyeing members to make sure their plates are piled high. If the church bans alcohol for health reasons, integrity demands that it also ban fried chicken.

Three Positions

The current Christian debate over alcohol centers around three positions: prohibition, abstention, and moderation. The prohibitionists insist that Christians cannot drink alcohol. Total abstention from alcohol is likely a condition for membership and baptism, and the consumption of alcohol by a member may result in disciplinary actions taken by the church. Abstentionists refuse to consume alcohol as the result of a personal moral stance, but do not attempt to force their opinion on others. They will not drink as a matter of conscience but have no objection to others who choose to drink. Those who choose moderation honor the Biblical cautions against drunkenness but freely engage in social drinking as they choose.

The Bible and the vast majority of church history support the position of moderation with one caveat. Christians should not use their freedoms in ways that will harm other Christians. "It is better not to eat meat or drink wine or to do anything else that will cause your brother or sister to fall" (Romans 14:21 NIV). This verse does not mean that people with narrow views on alcohol can dictate the behavior of people with more open views. Rather, it reminds us to put people over our appetites, a lesson I learned at a small wedding a few years ago. I happened to know that one of the members of the wedding party was an alcoholic who was leaving for rehab immediately following the wedding. At the reception, both champagne and non-alcoholic, sparking grape juice were offered. My wife and I decided to drink the grape juice, not because alcohol is evil, but to stand in solidarity with the woman who struggled with alcoholism. We didn't want our freedom to do any damage.

The Bible asserts that alcohol is a gift from God as long as we keep it in its proper place. It can add to a celebration, help us unwind after a long day, or even contribute certain health benefits in moderation. When it becomes more important than people, it can fuel arguments, break up families, cause people to drive carelessly, and even steal life away from us. It is a powerful force in our culture. Christians, who are called to love God and others, must treat it with respect.

6 A LINE IN THE SAND

Several years ago, my wife and I met a woman named Star at a local restaurant. She and her friends were enjoying dinner and drinks at the table next to us, and we struck up a conversation. The alcohol was flowing freely at their table, which probably encouraged her to share freely about herself. She had several tattoos and piercings, only some of which were visible. She told us the story of her first marriage and the divorce that followed. She was living with her current boyfriend who was at the table with her, and they shared a few stories that were "not safe for church." They lived what many in the church would call a wild life. During the conversation, someone at their table brought up the topic of polyamory. Star responded strongly with an expletive or two, "That's where I draw the line!"

It occurred to me that everybody has lines they won't cross. All people are moral according to their own codes of ethics. For some people, morality is a matter of personal standards. During our dinner conversation, Star broke most of the church rules of my youth, but she had standards that were important to her, moral viewpoints that guided her behavior. Her "morality" was separate from religion or any belief about God, but it was still vital to her in determining her own ethical living. For others, morality is based on cultural norms. They live their lives by the standards of what is culturally accepted in their time-period. One of the difficulties with this type of morality is that cultural standards are constantly changing. Two generations ago it was immoral for school teachers to marry. One generation ago, it was immoral for school teachers to be pregnant and "showing" at school. Today, such standards seem archaic, oppressive, even. For others, morality is rooted in religious belief. They attempt to behave in certain ways that honor God and their religious tradition. As we have seen in this book, though, developing a comprehensive list of morals from religious history is challenging at best. Even though they claim to believe the whole Bible, very few Christians want to live by Old Testament moral standards. Regardless of the source of ethics, everyone is moral—depending on where you draw the lines. And, it's good to have standards. Ethics give a meaningful shape to our lives and hopefully encourage us to live kindly with our fellow humans.

But, moralism doesn't save people. It doesn't even make them better Christians! "For it is by grace you have been saved, through faith—and this is not from yourselves, it is the gift of God—not by works, so that no one can boast" (Ephesians 2:8-9). Grace makes us right with God, and grace is a gift. It's love and acceptance that we don't deserve, and we can't earn. All of our attempts at morality do nothing to improve our standing with God. More amazingly, our failures do nothing to hurt our position with God! God doesn't save us because we're good, but because God is good! To add our morality to the equation is to imply that God's grace is not enough.

Just as our morality cannot make us Christian, neither can it make us better Christians. As Christ followers, our lives should increasingly resemble His, but this transformation is not accomplished through following lists of rules. Rather, our feeble attempts at morality actually get in the way! In the early church, Jewish Christians believed that Gentile converts to Christianity should be forced to honor God by following the hundreds of demands of the Jewish law. The Apostle Paul responded, "You who are trying to be justified by the law have been alienated from Christ; you have fallen away from grace" (Galatians 5:4 NIV). Attempting to follow Christ by following rules cuts us off from the grace that saved us. Morality has never been the pathway to God!

Throughout these six chapters, I've tried to illustrate the fallacy of morality. We've looked at the damaging effects of our rules about marriage and family, sexuality, profanity, and alcohol. We could add chapters on tattoos, piercings, smoking, horoscopes, magic, Ouija boards, horror movies, playing cards, and dancing. The list of prohibitions dreamed up by uptight church people seems interminable. Morality is a pale substitute for genuine Christianity. It is a false god that demands daily homage to arbitrary lists created by other immoral people. The church too often encourages people to be moral without teaching them to follow Christ. It also judges people who are following Christ for violating its arbitrary sense of morality. Neither position serves God or the individual.

Stripping away morality is threatening for many in the church. They assume that the absence of moralism means license to do anything we want, that the result will be debauchery, even anarchy. If we lose the safety of morality, what will guide our behavior? We'll address that question in part two.

PART TWO:

A BETTER WAY

7 THREE SIMPLE RULES

"Do not think that I have come to abolish the Law or the Prophets; I have not come to abolish them but to fulfill them.
Matthew 5:17

The end of the Law—it's a scary notion, especially for many of us who have grown up in the church. The Law keeps us safe. It tells us how to behave. It tells us who's on the inside (which always seems to be where *we* are) and who's on the outside. Life without the Law sounds risky, and immoral, and we fear it could lead to anarchy. So, I did what many Bible believing Christians did. I explained away this verse about Jesus fulfilling the Law. My explanation went something like this:

- All the Old Testament Law comes to the cross.
- Some of the law stops with Jesus' death, like ceremonial and dietary laws. On this point, my explanation relies on Acts 10, where Peter sees a vision of unclean foods and hears God's instructions to arise and eat. From this story, I assumed that all ceremonial and dietary laws are voided.
- Other parts of the law pass through the cross into the present unchanged, like prohibitions against lying or stealing.
- Still other parts of the Old Testament Law come to the cross and are modified. The Law forbids murder, but Jesus said that if you're angry at your brother or sister, you've

committed murder in your heart.

My explanation was a neat and tidy rationalization for someone who was addicted to morality. It allowed me the comfort of my lists of rules.

It's just not what the Bible says! First, no one in Jesus' day would have separated moral, ceremonial, and dietary law! It was THE Law, singular, one solitary unit, and Jesus finished it. The word for abolish in the above verse is *katalusai* in Greek which means overthrow or cancel, whereas the word for fulfill is *plerosai* which means complete or finish. Imagine a baseball game that goes into a rain delay in the third inning. If play cannot resume, the officials cancel the game *(katalusai)*. The game remains unfinished, incomplete. But, if play resumes through the ninth inning, and there is a winner, the game is completed *(plerosai)*. During time in the wilderness, Jesus was tempted three times to put His own interest above God's or other people's. He resisted. Through his obedience, he completed the demands of the Law for his own life. Through his death, and resurrection, Jesus brought the Law to its conclusion. He finished it and put something new in its place, what is often called the Great Commandment. "One of them, an expert in the law, tested him with this question: 'Teacher, which is the greatest commandment in the Law? Jesus replied: 'Love the Lord your God with all your heart and with all your soul and with all your mind.' This is the first and greatest commandment. And the second is like it: 'Love your neighbor as yourself.' All the Law and the Prophets hang on these two commandments" (Matthew 22:35-40 NIV). According to Jesus, the Law for Christians is love for God and others.

Biblical Love

As a child, I remember riding down the interstate with my family watching the world go by. I spotted a billboard that read, "The one who loves is born of God." It's a quote from the book of First John. "Dear friends, let us love one another, for love comes from God. Everyone who loves has been born of God and knows God. Whoever does not love does not know God, because God is love" (4:7-8 NIV). That thought put me at ease. Even as a young boy, I often wondered about heaven and whether I would get in. That afternoon, this simple verse gave me assurance. Anyone who loves knows God, and I could name at least two or three girls that I loved.

It wasn't until I was older that I learned about the three different words for love in the original language of the New Testament. First, is *eros* or romantic love. It's the root word for erotic. It's the love that I felt for those three girls. It's a wonderful gift of God that should be surrounded with celebration instead of shame. The love that connects us to God, though, runs even deeper. Second, is *philos*, which is friendship love. The third word for love in the New Testament is *agape*, which is unconditional love. It's the word used in John 3:16 to describe the way that God loves the *entire* world. It's also the word used in I John 4:7-8. My crush on those two or three girls was not evidence of salvation, nor were my one or two close friendships. *Agape* love is even more profound, but it's also risky! Jesus loved the outcasts of his day and even his enemies. His love was so far-reaching that the religious people couldn't tolerate it, and they killed him. People who follow Jesus have that same far-reaching love that encompasses even those people that church attenders too often condemn, and it's still as risky. That kind of love is the foundation of all Christian ethics and is the antithesis of moralism which tears at the very fiber of our faith. Moralism divides, judges, and condemns. It creates insiders and outsiders, winners and losers, or as C. S. Lewis puts it:

> People often think of Christian morality as a kind of bargain in which God says, "If you keep a lot of rules, I'll reward you, and if you don't I'll do the other thing." I do not think that is the best way of looking at it. I would much rather say that every time you make a choice you are turning the central part of you, the part of you that chooses, into something a little different from what it was before. And taking your life as a whole, with all your innumerable choices, all your life long you are slowly turning this central thing either into a Heavenly creature or a hellish creature; either into a creature that is in harmony with God, and other creatures, and with itself, or else into one that is in a state of war and hatred with God, and with its fellow creatures, and with itself (*The Joyful Christian*).

Choice by choice, Christian love embraces the entire world even as Christ did who came not to condemn the world but that the world, through Him, might be saved.

Three Simple Rules

Part two explores loving God and loving others in the light of three simple rules that will transform us into Heavenly creatures. They are part of the doctrinal standards of my denomination but are too often treated as historical artifacts rather that practical guidelines. I hope to resurrect them as the church's primary mode of operation in the world. The first rule is: do no harm. We'll consider it in Chapter 8. In Chapter 9, we'll explore the second rule: do all the good you can to all the people you can all the time that you can. Finally, in Chapter 10, we'll explore rule three: stay in love with God. As we begin this journey into unconditional love, I want to be audacious enough to offer another rule. Before rule number one, we Christians need to apologize for the harm the church has already done.

8 JUDGE NOT

Do not judge, or you too will be judged.
Jesus, *The Sermon on the Mount,*
Matthew 7:1

The kingdom of God is a party! Jesus repeatedly describes it as a feast, a banquet, and a wedding party. Jesus is the host of the party, and he offers an open invitation to *everyone* who will come. During his earthly ministry, Jesus included thieves (tax collectors), terrorists (zealots), lepers, prostitutes, the poor, and those with mental and physical challenges. In Luke 14, he insists that his house be full of partiers (v. 23), and Second Peter 3 reminds us that God doesn't want anyone to perish (v. 9). Jesus presented the faith as a way of loving the entire world.

How odd it is that among Jesus' so-called followers there are so many self-appointed bouncers, church people who stand by the door to carefully screen who is admitted to the party. They stand securely behind the velvet rope line appraising each would-be partier, evaluating appearance and behavior by an arbitrary list of rules developed by some aloof board or council. Only those who meet the standard are admitted, and if anyone inside breaks the rules, the bouncers are on the spot to eject the troublemaker. For centuries, this evil game seemed to be effective. The church maintained order, by force when necessary, even torturing people into compliance—all for the safety of their souls, of course.

The culture no longer plays the game. In recent decades, people have seen through the hypocrisy of our religion, and they are opting out in record numbers. According to the Barna Research Group, 77% of unchurched people in America are people who were once in church and have left. There are 30.8 million Americans who were once a part of a church but walked away. Among them are some famous names.

Brad Pitt was raised in a Christian home where faith was a central part of his life. But, Beliefnet.com reports, "In 2007, Pitt admitted [during an interview with *Parade* Magazine] to a 'crisis of faith' in high school. 'I'd go to Christian revivals and be moved by the Holy Spirit,' Pitt said, 'And I'd go to rock concerts and feel the same fervor. Then I'd be told, 'That's the devil's music! Don't partake in that!' I wanted to experience things religion said not to experience.'" Rules ran Pitt out of the faith, and he now considers himself an atheist.

According to the same article, Katy Perry is the daughter of two Christian ministers and began her career in Christian music. She eventually left the faith citing, "her strict upbringing, and the confining nature of Christianity as a part of the reason she has left it." Confining nature sounds dramatically different from the freedom that comes in Jesus (John 8:36). The article goes on to discuss Gabriel Byrne who answered a call to ministry and began his studies in seminary. His time in ministry and the church was cut short when a member of the clergy sexually abused him. He now compares the church to Nazi Germany. The article continues to tell the stories of other actors who have left the faith including Julia Roberts, Hugh Laurie, and Bruce Willis, and then it predictably blames *them* and their fame for their failures. Even though the actors explain the role that moralism, and in Byrne's case evil acts by clergy, played in their decisions to walk away, Beliefnet refuses to consider that the church might be the problem.

It's not just the famous who are experiencing this crisis of faith. According to Barna, "Only about one in ten adults [in The United States] have never attended a Christian church at any time in his or her life, other than for a special service such as a wedding or funeral ceremony. The majority of unchurched individuals have firsthand experience with one or more Christian churches and, based on that sampling, have decided they can better use their time in other ways" (Barna 36). Most of the American unchurched have been to church and left, and the church's kneejerk reaction is to blame them for leaving. Church goers tend to demonize those who no longer want to be a part, accusing them of weak faith or of falling into sin. Rarely is the church honest enough with itself to admit its own abuses. In my experience, the vast majority of people who leave the church leave with good reason. They were hurt over issues that are not central to the Gospel! Of course, there are exceptions.

Time to Take a Stand

Sometimes, people leave the church because it

takes a necessary stand. It's sad to see people walk away, but the church can't sacrifice legitimate values in an effort to keep people from leaving. While serving a previous church, a couple made an appointment with me to share some serious concerns they had about our ministry. When we met, they asked if I would allow homosexuals to worship with us. I assured them that I would welcome them. Upon hearing my response, the couple announced that they could not worship with homosexuals, and if I was going to allow it, then they would leave. I took a stand for love and acceptance, and the couple kept their promise. They left and never returned. They found a home in a different congregation that supported their bigotry. Sometimes, people leave because the church did the right thing. I remember one Sunday morning in another church when two African-American men walked into our all white congregation. Upon their entrance, a man in the back of the room got up and left in protest. Sadly, a loving welcome to all people still excludes some, but they are excluded because of their own hatred. This particular fellow came back the following week to continue to fight for his hatred. The church should never violate the law of love in an effort to gain or retain members!

Understanding the Pain

Too many of the 30.8 million people who left the church left with good reasons. They left because the church did spiritual violence to their souls. They left because of unrealistic rules that have no foundation in Christ's teachings. They left because of the church's failure to love. They suffer from what has become known as Post Traumatic Church Syndrome (PTCS).

While not listed in the DSM5, this condition is a reality for many who have been hurt by the church. Author and blogger Dr. Benjamin Corey describes it this way. "People with PTCS have in one way or another, been wounded by the very place they went to seek healing. These wounds create an emotional barrier for a person to engage in church, create barriers for them to connect with God, and create barriers for people to develop authentic community with other followers of Jesus." The church needs to quit defending itself. It needs to quit blaming those who have left because of pain the church inflicted. It's time for the church to own its part of the story.

In short, the church needs to confess and repent. That message is normally the one we in the church preach to a "lost world," but perhaps it's the church that has lost its way. If confession is as good as we say, we should try it. I wish I could speak for the whole church, but as an ordained pastor, I want to apologize to the thousands of victims of religious moralism, spiritual violence, and abuse. I'm sorry for the ways I've contributed to it, and I'm sorry for the pain done by my colleagues and constituents. I'm even more sorry that, in some places, the abuse will likely continue for the foreseeable future. If you're a victim, I understand your caution in coming back. I pray you can find a church that will love you because I know a God who certainly does. So, to all of those who we've hurt, I confess. To those of us in the church, we have to stop hurting people in the name of Jesus! We betray our Lord with our hatred!

My Sin

I'm guilty. I'm one of the ones who has done the

damage. More than ten years ago, a wonderful woman in one of my churches came to visit me. She told me that two of her three sons were gay. I shared with her that I loved her boys and that they were welcome in our church. I also told her that her sons' homosexual relationships were not God's best for them. I was proud of myself for saying that I loved them, proud that I would let "those people" worship in my church. But, I was blind to the unnecessary pain I caused this mother. For years, I was oblivious until recently when she sent me a Facebook message on the occasion of the wedding of my daughter, Katherine, to her wife, Hannah. The message was a dagger into my heart. After congratulating my daughter and daughter-in-law on their wedding, she continued to say, "I also hope that they will not have to endure the hardship of a pastor that tells them they are not God's best work which are the words you spoke to me and about my family. Those words caused so much damage to my heart that I cannot go without speaking them as you spoke them to me." Her words shattered me. I couldn't bear the reality of my own hatefulness. Immediately, I responded, "It's good to hear from you! I hope that you and your family are doing great. Thank you for your kind words for Katherine and Hannah. They are deeply in love, and we have the pleasure of them living with us while Katherine finishes her master's degree. I couldn't be prouder of Hannah. I have confessed my hateful statements of the past to God and my congregations over the last several years. I regret that I have not contacted you directly to confess to you! I hope you'll forgive me. My understanding of human sexuality and scripture has certainly evolved over the years. I'm grateful to you for pushing me when I was your pastor. Your questions led me to deeper digging into the scriptures, which has led me to a place of inclusiveness. It's been too long a journey, but I'm grateful to be where I am living with and serving with an ever-broadening diversity of God's children. I love you and your family! May God bless you all abundantly."

I never meant to do harm. I thought I was being faithful to scripture. I discovered in my own story the danger of making pronouncements and enforcing rules when I hadn't done due diligence in wrestling with the issues. Before we presume to speak on behalf of God, we better make damn sure that we know God's opinion!

My story is an isolated example of a pervasive problem. The church has done too much damage to too many people. It's time to stop hurting people in the name of Jesus. Throughout the remainder of this chapter, I'll address at least four areas where the church needs to stop harming people.

The church needs to stop sending people to hell.

Rev. Billy Graham got it right. "It's the Holy Spirit's job to convict, God's job to judge, and my job is to love." The church confuses those roles too often. In its rush to honor scripture, evangelical Christianity is committing blasphemy by taking authority to do what is reserved for the Holy Spirit. When the church convicts and judges, it's not serving God, but playing God, and people are suffering because of its sin. Mary is one of their victims. When she found out I was writing this book, she wrote to share her story.

A year and a half ago I lost my sister to suicide. It was a really difficult time for us and still is, and we have had a hard time dealing with criticism from Christians who are often insensitive about how my sister passed away. One blatantly told me that my sister is going to hell. It's very difficult to hear that "only God can take a life" when I know how much my sister suffered during her final years. She started getting sick right after the birth of her daughter (she was also a single parent) and it was heartbreaking to see her deterioration (post-partum depression). She got to a point where she couldn't even bathe herself anymore. I know it sounds crazy to say, but a part of us is relieved that she is no longer suffering. I believe that if God is really a God of love, that surely my sister would be in a place now where she is free from her suffering and not "burning" for not being able to continue on any longer. This kind of judgment is also why people choose to refrain from speaking up about mental illness and we have this big issue with not only stigma from others, but self-stigma, too. She left behind a now 8-year old daughter who I will be adopting soon, and it's hard for me when my niece asks about Jesus. Right now, Jesus makes her happy, so I am more than willing to teach her all about him, but I just hope she stays in it for Jesus and the right reasons and not to think that she is better than others - a vibe most "Christians" in my life give off.

Condemning her sister to hell—I wish I could say I was surprised. God alone is judge, and he is more merciful than we can imagine. The judgement Mary faced from the church was pure evil resulting from someone's irresponsible, half-witted attempt at interpreting scripture. I'm amazed at Mary's willingness to continue to teach her niece about Jesus after the way "Christians" treated her. She exhibits more grace than the religious crowd around her. Still, the abuse has taken a toll on her. She continues.

> I am honestly not sure if I believe in God anymore. I used to, but my faith in Christianity has been shattered, because I used to see the same people at church every Sunday (knowing full well that they are having extra-marital affairs or stealing money and committing fraud). I like to think there is a stronger force/karma/the Universe that holds people accountable for their actions, but I am still trying to figure it all out for myself.

I can't help but wonder what the difference in Mary's life would have been if the church had showed up in her time of grief with love and open arms instead of pointing fingers.

Some of us Christians derive too much pleasure from the idea of people burning in hell for eternity. In *Love Wins*, Christian pastor Rob Bell simply questioned whether God might save everyone in the end, and the Christian world rose up against him. To this day, many consider him a heretic for simply suggesting that eternal torture might not exist. Our eagerness to toss people into hell runs counter to the heart of Christ who came for the redemption of the world! I pray regularly that God has a plan to bring all of humanity home.

The church needs to stop abusing women.

During my research for this book, I asked unchurched friends to share their stories about how the church hurt them. Not surprisingly, all the stories I received came from women. To be fair, it wasn't a large enough sample to draw scientific conclusions, and there might be many reasons why women would be more likely to share. Still, the results of my informal survey remind me that it's easy to be a straight, white man in the church. For women, it's an entirely different story.

My friend Ann told me that merely walking into a church building makes her physically sick due to years of abuse she suffered in the church world. Ann grew up in a church that taught her that God is love. In that church, she felt loved and accepted and saw God as a loving father-figure. That positive view of God was shattered after her marriage and initiation into her husband's church. Ann told me that her new church was very dualistic with lots of rules. She said, "They made me feel like everyone was cookie-cutter, and I didn't belong, because I didn't conform to their way of doing things." It was a very male dominated church where women were to be seen and not heard. When Ann's husband was being considered for deacon, she was told that her job would be to "shut up and mind." The men of the church controlled the entirety of the women and children's lives. Children attended the church's school where they could be indoctrinated in church ways. Even there, the boys enjoyed a favored position. One day when Ann stopped by the school at lunch, she witnessed a boy slam her daughter's face into the table in full view of the male administrator. When he didn't take any action, Ann questioned him about the boy's behavior. The administrator conveniently claimed that he didn't see anything. The misogyny even extended to the females' dress code. Girls could only wear shorts if they fell well below the knees, and women were required to wear ankle length dresses. For Ann, church became a barrier to God rather than a path to God. She came to believe that God was angry at her for being herself. She was convinced that, if she could get to heaven, St. Peter would show her what a piece of crap she was. Years after escaping from an abusive marriage and a hateful church, she still feels the separation from God. She said, "For a lot of years, hatefulness and God were the same thing."

For too long, churches have twisted the words of scripture to justify mistreatment of women. The Bible gives specific instructions for specific contexts, and they have been generalized in an effort to marginalize women. Most chauvinists can misrepresent a Bible verse or two about women being silent in church. Those men are not seeking Biblical holiness but the oppression of women. Instead, Christians should celebrate stories of women leaders in the church like Lydia, who oversaw the church at Philippi, Pheobe a deacon and minister to Rome, and Pricilla who instructed Apollos. Many of Jesus' followers were women, and some supported his ministry financially. In all four Gospels, the first preacher of the resurrection was a woman. Of course, the New Testament events occurred in paternalistic times and were recorded by paternalistic authors. Even so, taken as a whole, the New Testament's view of women is better represented by Paul's statement in Galatians 3. "There is neither Jew nor Gentile, neither slave nor free, nor is there male and female, for you are all one in Christ Jesus" (v. 28). Christian teaching that bashes women also bashes Christ!

The Church needs to stop demonizing sexuality.

Church folks are obsessed with sex. They're afraid someone might be having sex. Worse yet, they're afraid someone might be enjoying sex. In the church's mind, the worst kinds of sin are sexual. Twenty-two men on a football field giving one another concussions is wholesome entertainment, but the Sports Illustrated Swimsuit edition is scandalous. According to Benjamin Corey, 75% of human trafficking is done for cheap labor so that we can have cheap products like milk chocolate. There is no outcry from the church about those practices. The only outrage I've heard from the church is over the 25% of human trafficking that is sex trafficking. Child laborers live in cages so we can eat cheap candy, and the church doesn't notice, but it stands ready to attack the sex industry. The church's attack on human trafficking is dripping with hypocrisy. Pastors are celebrated for being hateful toward women, homosexuals, immigrants, and other races, but their careers end over a sexual indiscretion. I don't know if it's relevant, but Hawkeye Pierce of M*A*S*H suggests that maybe our preoccupation with sex comes from a lack of occupation with sex. Whatever the reason for our obsession, the reality is that our teaching on sex stinks. It's horrible. The only church instruction I ever received on sex was, "Don't." It's not surprising that throughout my ministry I have seen countless marriages that suffered in various ways from unsatisfactory sex lives.

Our bad teaching starts early. My friend, Alicia, a twenty-four-year-old woman recently shared with me.

"When I was about 10-11, I was in Sunday school and my teacher said, 'Sex of all kinds is wrong, but someone's gotta do it [for procreation].' When I was 10, I had heard about sex, but I didn't fully grasp the concept of it or really "get" it. Several years later, when I fully understood what it was and thought back about that time, I was like 'really? Sex is JUST for procreating and NOTHING else?' Growing up in a church that suppressed any sort of sexuality actually made me SCARED of sex and of my body." Not surprisingly, Alicia is no longer active in church. Her story could be told a thousand times over because the church has perpetuated this lie for decades. The truth is in the mind of the Creator. God created sex for procreation AND for pleasure. The fact is indisputable by the way that God designed us. Females bear the brunt of the "procreation only" lie, but God designed their bodies specifically for pleasure as well as procreation. The clitoris has 8000 nerve endings, more than any other part of the human body (male or female), and its sole purpose is pleasure (Thomason). God designed sex for pleasure, and the church's bad teaching has been robbing people of joy for centuries.

Natalie, a one-time minister, provides another powerful example of a young woman driven away from church by sexual repression. The "purity" message was a central theme while she was in college. She shared some of her experience with me.

While attending a very vibrant church in university the purity message was driven hard. In one of the lessons I vividly recall, the entire sermon (followed by reinforcement through cell groups etc.) was that masturbation is self-sex, and therefore the same level of sin as having sex with someone before marriage. To avoid stumbling into this sinful behavior that we would need to give account for on THAT day (judgement day) we needed to avoid any sexual thoughts, and when we found our minds wandering, the thing to do was to "bounce your thoughts" to something else.

This negative message about sexuality sounds all too familiar. I heard a youth pastor interpret Jesus' words, "And if your right hand causes you to stumble, cut it off and throw it away" (Matthew 5:30a) as a prohibition against masturbation. Talk about church induced guilt! Natalie proceeded to tell me that female college students were made to feel responsible for the men's sexual purity, so they had to be careful "not to make our brothers stumble." Marriage was exalted as a blood-covenant confirmed in the breaking of the hymen making virginity a rigid requirement for the females (not so much for the males). The teaching Natalie endured made dating and even friendships almost impossible. She continues.

It also created a level of dysfunction in friendships in the church. Because if you were attracted to someone, you had to keep in mind that they might be "somebody else's future spouse" so you should not think about them in a way that their future spouse might not be happy with. And because it would be akin to mentally cheating on your own future spouse.

Like Alicia, the church taught Natalie the evils of sex, even for married women.

Once my female friends got married, there was the

next challenge of - how to let yourself enjoy sex that was so sinful, but now suddenly it's OK. Most of the women I spoke with said that it was something that they just "got on with" because they knew their husbands had been waiting for so long, but that they hated themselves after, and felt dirty. It was also a very unpleasant experience for most women, and when they would come back from honeymoon and mention this to other married women, their response was unanimously - yeah, we didn't want to tell you it was going to be awful. But it always starts that way.

While there are certain emotional and physical risks involved with sex, the church's message on the evils of sex has done much spiritual, emotional, and physical damage. For Natalie, the result of the purity message was physical pain.

When I did become sexually active again it was excruciatingly painful. I went to specialist upon specialist until eventually my gynecologist suggested I go to a pelvic physiotherapists. The 1st thing she asked me was if I was religious. When I responded in the affirmative, she told me that in her practice over 80% of the time, when women come in for painful sex it is because they have a religious background, about 10% is because of past abuse, and the rest are various physiological reasons. Those numbers horrified me. After 3 sessions, and MANY tears, I can now have pain free intercourse. But it is not without a lot of concentration on many days. Concentrating on relaxing, reminding myself that enjoying sex doesn't make me a slut, and it's ok to welcome my partner to me. Allowing myself to trust.

Eventually, Natalie left the ministry. Now, she and a friend are working to help other women experience healthy relationships, but she hasn't yet escaped the reach of the church.

A good friend and I have both come to a balance with embracing both our faith and sexual selves, and we both worked for the same church previously. Whenever we meet we have hysterical conversations around dating, relationship and sex faux pas. We really want to start a podcast to cover some heavy topics on those themes in a lighthearted way. The one thing holding us back: all of our church friends would then know about our "other lives" where we date and make mistakes. And we know that we would either be called in for "friendly chats" or cut off from friends who don't want to be tainted by association.

I pray for the day when the church is ready for such podcasts, for a time when the church will be proactive in teaching people about their bodies, these wonderful gifts from our Creator. I hope for a time when part of pre-marital and marriage counseling is teaching and encouraging couples to have mind-blowing sex. I dream of marriage enrichment retreats that aren't afraid to discuss fulfilling sex lives. Until the church learns to encourage healthy sexuality, I fear that I'll spend more time helping people heal from painful divorces.

The church needs to stop telling people who they can love.

I attended a church meeting shortly after the U. S. Supreme Court legalized same-sex marriage. This particular gathering was exclusively for people who had attended a spiritual retreat that focused on God's unconditional love. While going through the buffet line, I overheard two men discussing the court's decision. According to them, "If God doesn't punish America for supporting same-sex marriage, He owes Sodom and Gomorrah and apology." I shared with them what Ezekiel said about Sodom, that it was their greed that caused their destruction, but I was even more amazed at the complete lack of logic in their argument. Europeans came to this continent and displaced Native Americans by violence. Our forefathers marched them off of their lands murdering thousands along the way. For much of our history, we enslaved African-Americans, and once they were freed from slavery, we caged them behind walls of separate but very unequal segregation. In the World War II era, we sent shiploads of refugees back to Germany to be slaughtered in Nazi death camps, while we imprisoned Asian U. S. citizens in our own concentration camps. We refused the right to vote to women and African-Americans. When the latter insisted on their rights, we turned fire hoses on them, turned dogs loose on them, lynched them, and murdered them as they peacefully marched for freedom. For 239 years, God showed this country mercy in spite of our blood-soaked history, but, according to these two churchmen, God was due to destroy us because we allowed people who love each other to marry.

Some think that homosexuality is an act of rebellion, but, again, the logic fails. All the homosexuals I've known faced negative consequences because of their orientation. They've endured name-calling and slurs. They've been rejected by family members, even parents. Unable to live with the rejection, too many have committed suicide. These are not rebels. No one chooses to go through the difficulty associated with homosexuality in this culture! The church must stop telling people who they can love. We've already hurt too many people, people like Iva.

When Iva learned that I was writing on the "fallacy of morality," she immediately volunteered to share her story with you.

I was born in 1956 and grew up in a small rural town in North Carolina. Raised in the Baptist church, I loved the "love of God" and felt the comfort of that until I was about 5 or 6, when they decided it was time for all the little kids to realize the need to "repent." I thought God was love and I thought I was living in that and could not understand what I could possibly be doing wrong that I had to repent for. Was I supposed to do something "wrong" so God could see that I was appealing to him when I did repent??? I did not understand. I also did not understand the hatred of people of color or homosexuality that was being promoted in this church.

As I grew up, it was difficult to relate to the church. Even after leaving the church at about the age of 15, I still had this voyeuristic god following me around. After enjoying the freedom and intellectual stimulation of college, I dropped out early, because I felt guilty about following my passions of music, finding a wonderful romantic experience with a woman and basically enjoying life. I thought God was going to throw me into hell. I did not realize that I was about to create a hell for myself. I dropped out of college, left my lovely woman and proceeded to spend the next 35 years desperately seeking that man I was supposed to marry to be happy and right in the eyes of God. Trying hard to be someone I wasn't was painful. I have finally started to step into my true self, my sexuality, my spiritual connection. And quite frankly, I don't think I'll ever set foot in a church without feeling uncomfortable.

In the church's blind rush to save people from hell it drove Iva right into her own church-created hell and cut her off from the very group of people who should demonstrate the unconditional love of God.

Many in today's church continue to insist that their objection to homosexuality is based on Biblical authority, but that argument is a red herring. The same Biblical Christians are not taking a stand against greedy people, or lawyers, or bankers, or people who eat meat with the blood still in it, even though the Bible specifically prohibits greed (I Cor. 6:10), taking legal action (I Cor. 6:7), charging interest (Deut. 23:19), and eating medium-rare steaks (Acts 15:20). The Biblical argument is an excuse to exclude people they don't like.

When logic finally fails, the response of last resort is typically, "Well, it's just gross to think about them having sex." If they're honest, the same can be said of quite a few heterosexual couples. Distaste for something doesn't make it evil.

Jesus' harshest words were reserved not for foreign occupying forces, but for the Pharisees who "were confident of their own righteousness and looked down on everyone else" (Luke 18:9 NIV). We follow in their footsteps when we trust in our own positions while demonizing others. When we require more of people than the Bible requires, we join the Pharisees in putting heavy burdens on other people's shoulders that we, ourselves, are not willing to lift (Matthew 23:4).

Obviously, it's impossible to discuss all the areas of potential harm. The ones in this chapter reflect the stories I've heard. I am still collecting and sharing stories. If you have one to tell, please consider sending it to me at DoctorK223@gmail.com.

Every time we fail to love God and neighbor, we do harm. That fact leads to the second rule. Do all the good that you can!

9 TREAT PEOPLE RIGHT

*"And whoever in the name of a disciple gives to one of these
little ones even a cup of cold water to drink, truly I say to you,
he shall not lose his reward."*

Jesus, Matthew 10:42 NASB

For centuries, the Hebrew people struggled
under the impossible weight of the 613 laws of the
Torah. Encoded in this dense rulebook were laws
about eating, drinking, cleanliness, relationships, sex,
and worship. They included prohibitions against
eating pork, mixing meat and dairy, wearing blended
fabrics, touching a menstruating woman, and doing
any kind of work on the Sabbath including writing
and erasing. It was impossible to follow all the rules
all the time, and the punishment for breaking them
could be severe—even death. By the time Jesus began
his ministry, much of this once vibrant religion had
eroded into moralism. Religion was all about the Law.
So, Jesus replaced 613 rules with two. Love God with
our entire lives, and love others as we love ourselves.
According to Jesus, by following these two
commandments people could be faithful to the entire
Law. Love God. Love others. Period.

Love is Action!

Biblically speaking, love is not an emotion. It doesn't describe the way that we feel about a person or the butterflies fluttering in our stomachs when we encounter the object of our affection. It's not a sensation that grows and fades with our circumstances. In the Bible, love is an action, a verb. Simply said, love is treating people right. When considered in this light, it's easier to understand how Jesus could require us to love our enemies. His instruction doesn't require us to conjure up warm, fuzzy feelings for people that we don't even like. Instead, he calls us to treat people right, with dignity and respect, regardless of the way we feel about them. In spite of differences and disagreements, we can treat people right.

It's the way our lesbian friends from chapter three treated me. During the week that we camped side-by-side, we never discussed their sexuality, and I certainly never mentioned my theological objections to it. While I acted aloof, due to my own bigotry, they treated me with love and respect. They shared their resources with me. They were generous to my family. They loved, even though I'm certain they sensed my judgmentalism, and their love broke through my self-righteous walls. In the presence of genuine, deep love, disagreements faded away.

The mark of a Christian is not some arbitrary moral standard, but love! The Apostle John underscores the significance of active love in a Christ followers life. "If anyone has material possessions and sees a brother or sister in need but has no pity on them, how can the love of God be in that person? Dear children, let us not love with words or speech but with actions and in truth" (I John 3:17-18). Nicole shared a beautiful story of just this kind of active love. Even though the church rejected Nicole because of her profession as a bartender, she persisted in following Christ and was active in the small group that met at my house. She loves like Jesus.

So, last night we went out after work, and at this particular bar in Kennesaw you have to pass the dance floor to get to the restroom. So, as I'm walking out of the restroom I notice this guy dancing all by himself (it was very apparent that he had a mental disability) and a group of REALLY pretty girls dancing, and you could see him get closer, and they would move their little circle away. Well, this just wasn't okay with me. I grabbed his hands, and we danced for the next half hour, and, let me just say, some his moves weren't so smooth, but I followed suit and he would laugh and clap; my heart melted. I had more fun dancing with him than I've ever had with anyone else. People could tell how much fun we were having and joined, and he made friends. A couple of people came to me and told me how awesome what I did was, and I told them, "Thank you, but just pass it on, do it for someone else." I didn't want to dance, I just got off work and was cramping like crazy, but he just wanted to feel accepted and dance with friends, best feeling ever to see his face light up. I guess moral of my story is don't be that group of girls, go dance and make someone's night.

Christian love does all the good that it can all the time that it can to all the people it can. It also loves deeply enough to offer help that is helpful.

Unhelpful Help

An episode of M*A*S*H illustrates unhelpful help. During his first Christmas in Korea, the wealthy Major Charles Emerson Winchester III continues a family tradition of anonymously buying gourmet chocolate candy for the poor children of a local orphanage. Later in the episode, Dr. Winchester discovers that the delicacies were sold on the black market. Outraged, Charles confronts the director of the orphanage about his misuse of the gift and, even worse, his violation of Winchester family tradition. The orphanage director gently responds that the major's generous gift would have been a special treat for Christmas morning, but on the black market, it brought enough money to buy the children food for a month. Major Winchester's gift was about him more than it was the children.

It's easy to give like the major when we discover the disparity between our relative wealth and the scarcity of our neighbors. When confronted with poverty and social injustices, we may feel compelled to action, but sometimes our helping does little more than soothe our consciences. Our attempts to help may miss the mark because we don't understand the issue, because we throw cash at a problem, or because, in our arrogance, we assume that we know what's best for people.

Sometimes, our efforts to help remind me of the proverbial Boy Scout helping the lady across a street she never intended to cross. We make efforts that seem good to us without investing the time required to understand the complexity of the issue. People often assume the best help for someone in poverty is a job. The church I serve currently employs people living in poverty to do work that we need and to help improve their situations. But, we have to be careful that our helping doesn't hurt. Imagine Sue, a 28-year-old single mom with two children. The federal poverty level for her family is $20,420. Food assistance is based on 130% of that amount or $26,546. Health care and other benefits are figured at 138% of the poverty level or $28,179. If Sue is at the upper limit, her gross monthly pay is $2,348. After taxes, that amount has to cover at least housing, utilities, food, school expenses, transportation, and healthcare. To help with that formidable task, she receives hundreds of dollars per month in food assistance, housing, and health insurance subsidies. If we try to help by increasing her pay by a few dollars per paycheck, she loses hundreds of dollars in benefits. Sue wants to be independent of government assistance, but the gap between her current pay and sufficient income to cover necessities is simply too wide. It's a complex problem that will require a complex solution, but it highlights the fact that our well-meaning but misguided efforts can do more harm than good. Encouraging people to "get a job" is not the answer.

In an affluent culture, the easiest way to try to help is giving money. Most of us have more money than time, and we're too often reluctant to spend precious time investing in the lives of strangers. Often our financial gifts don't help, and sometimes they even hurt. During 30 years of ministry, I've encountered hundreds of people asking cash for a variety of crises: rent, utilities, food, medical, gasoline, etc. Some of the requests are legitimate. Many are not, and it's nearly impossible to discern the difference. As a rule, I don't give cash. There's too high a risk that it will be used to feed addictions or simply misused. Rarely is money a genuine help, but people give it because it's easy. Handing a $5 bill out the car window to the man on the street corner doesn't cost much, and that simple gift assures us that we've done a good deed. In reality, it's a substitute for real help, and it encourages people to become dependent on charitable agencies for life's necessities. Genuine help may require our money, but it also requires our time and our investment in other people's lives with the goal of helping people become financially independent contributors to society.

When dealing with injustice, it's easy to assume that we know best. As a teenager, I spent an afternoon volunteering at a camp for children with physical challenges. While there, I saw a camper pick up a boy with no legs and put him on the back of a water fountain to get a drink. What appeared to be a good deed quickly horrified me when the camper ran off, leaving the boy with no legs stranded on a ledge, four feet off the ground. Moved by compassion, I went to help the boy down, but before I could get there, he jumped to the floor and ran away on his hands to his next adventure. I stood there shocked that he wasn't as limited as I assumed he was. Part of doing all the good that we can is building enough of a relationship that we understand what is truly good. It's difficult to help people we don't know.

Do the Good that you Can

At its most basic level, doing good is not complicated. Know your community. Build relationships with people. Meet the needs you can.

While volunteering at a local community service agency, Mandy received a request from a young mother for an electric space heater. That night, the temperatures would drop dangerously low, and the young woman had no way to keep herself and her children warm. The agency had no heaters, but Mandy found blankets for the young family. Because Mandy took the initiative to be involved in her community, she became aware of the need. Because she knew her county, she understood that there was much substandard housing where the electricity to run space heaters was not a given. The situation moved her. She did what she could, and *Blanket Cleburne* was born. Since that cold winter night, Mandy has given away hundreds of blankets to residents of Cleburne County and beyond.

Cold weather was not the only threat to the people of Cleburne County. Many residents drive more than 20 minutes to the closest grocery store. The unavailability of food combined with the high poverty rate and the cost of transportation makes the community a "food desert." Church leaders in the community discovered that they had access to affordable food through one of the state food banks. They saw a need. They did what they could, and *Feeding Cleburne* was born. Last month, *Feeding Cleburne* provided groceries to over 400 households in a county of 15,000 people. It's not hard to do good, but it does require time, sacrifice, and building relationships.

I was privileged to watch a group of about a dozen teenagers make their mark on the world. During a meeting at church, they discovered that over five million children under the age of five die each year from hunger and hunger-related disease. That group of teens decided to make a difference. They partnered with a reputable agency. They worked fund-raisers. They experienced hunger and homelessness by fasting for 30 hours while living outdoors in cardboard boxes. Through their efforts, they raised enough money to provide food, water, education, and medical care for 8 children for one year! During their fast, all the students shared that going without food was more difficult than they had imagined, but it was worth the effort to save children's lives.

In my current church, Christ followers consistently demonstrate God's unconditional love. Every day of the week, our volunteers mentor students at our elementary school, improving their chances of graduation. One week each month, they support patients and families at hospice during some of the most difficult times of life. Our members volunteer with veterans, serve in a free health clinic, and at the hospital. They live out the truth that following Jesus means doing good to other human beings.

To be honest, doing the right thing is not always pleasant. As winter approached, my church decided to help winterize homes in a poor part of our community. We met with residents requesting help, gathered supplies, and set out early one Saturday morning to love our neighbors. The plan was to cover single pane windows with plastic and to put weather stripping around doors. During the morning, we entered one home that needed far more. From the doorway of the bathroom, we could see the ground beneath the floor. The floor needed to be replaced. With the homeowner's permission, we gathered more supplies and tools and went to work. Because of the deterioration of the floor, the toilet had become disconnected from the sewage line. I remember lying on the ground and using my foot to push the sewage pipe back into place so that my partner could reconnect it. As I lay on the ground in the cold and sewage, I offered up a very honest prayer. I told God that this kind of work was not what I had in mind when I entered ministry. I imagined myself in fine robes speaking to massive crowds, garnering the respect of everyone in the community. Sewage was never a part of my plan. God responded very clearly to me that this is what Christ-like love looks like. It was part of God's plan.

Doing good will, occasionally, lead to opposition. Our church learned that two high school girls in our community were pregnant. Both attended the same church, a church that only shamed them for the sin of premarital sex. So, our church offered to throw them a baby shower. We decorated with fine linens, silver and crystal. The ladies of the church provided their best delicacies, and our members showed up with presents in hand. We invited not only the moms-to-be, but also the dads-to-be. It was a great celebration. However, after the party, a lady in the community cornered me. "I just don't believe it's right throwing a shower for pregnant teenagers. Showers are just for the couples that do it right. You're encouraging bad behavior." I responded, "We're showing love. It's hard to be teen parents, and they need to feel the love and support of the church, not its judgement! Furthermore, I don't believe any teenage girl is intentionally going to get pregnant so that she can have a party where the gifts are baby bottles and diapers." She didn't like my response, and I'm okay with that.

Doing good is about loving people, no matter what. In chapter four, I introduced you to Terry who lived in the broken-down trailer behind one of my churches. I told you about how my small group befriended him. There's more to the story. The night we introduced him to the group, one of my group members taught me a lesson I hope I never forget. Our plan was to take Terry out to a nice restaurant for dinner, but he wanted a shower first. Angie, a lady in our group, owned a hair salon that happened to have a full bathroom with a shower, and she agreed to let Terry get ready for dinner at her shop and even included a haircut. It was my job to get him there, and that meant picking him up in my car, my nice car with clean, cloth seats. I confess that I worried about the odor and the stain that he might leave in my Accord. I knew I was doing good, but I also had reservations. Still, I picked Terry up and took him to the shop, and yes, there was an odor. When we arrived at the shop, Angie crossed the floor and gave this dirty, smelly stranger the biggest hug you can imagine. I stood there in awe of Angie's love for him and in shame of my concern for my car. What a beautiful expression of love.

Do all the good that you can to all the people that you can all the time that you can. One time it's a blanket. Another time, it's a bag of groceries. Still another time, it might be home repairs. Or, doing good might just mean a kind word or a hug. In order to follow Christ, we must love people deeply and unconditionally!

We must also stay in love with God.

10 FOR THE LOVE OF GOD

Love the Lord your God with all your heart and with all your soul and with all your strength.

Deuteronomy 6:5

Christ followers treat people right, but they're not the only ones who treat others with love and respect. The church must honor people, but it also must connect with God. It should be distinguished not only by the way it treats people but also by how it connects to God. To be authentic, the church must be innately spiritual. In an organization consumed with moralism, the spirit withers and dies, and that truth has been the case too often in North American Christianity. Moralistic churches are like the husband who buys his wife a Valentine's Day present only to stay out of trouble. Spiritual churches are more like the husband who buys that present because he is head over hills, deeply, intimately in love with his wife. Many people have left the church because of abuse, but others left because of spiritual malnutrition. Shannon wrote to tell me her story.

I was a member of the United Church of Canada growing up, and really, really wanted to be a Christian, in the true sense of Christ as Lord and Savior, etc. vs attending church. I felt it just didn't take for me, and I did not have, and do not have faith or belief it could happen, but I moved on to be *more spiritual*, with a *neo-pagan* twist I suppose, largely believing that there is something larger than myself, interconnectedness between us all. (Italics added.)

Shannon's story is a wake-up call for the church for whom spirituality is supposed to be a strength. Yet, I have talked with many people who left our Christian sanctuaries to find spiritual meaning in other places. The church doesn't exist to make people behave. It exists to foster a relationship with the living God, and it's time to get back to those basics.

God longs for a deep, interpersonal relationship with people. Hosea 4:6 states that God's people are destroyed for a lack of knowledge. God is not saying that people are destroyed for not knowing enough facts about God, the Bible or religion. This destruction is not due to a lack of information but a lack of intimacy. In the original language of Hebrew, the word for knowledge is *daath*. It is the same root word as the word knew, *yada*, in Genesis 4:1 which says that Adam knew his wife. The result of that knowledge was pregnancy. The entire book of Hosea illustrates God's desire for an intimate relationship with people. Orthodoxy without intimacy leads to destruction. God invites us to fall in love.

There are hundreds of ways that people might connect with God: music, friendships, nature walks, holding a newborn baby, and the list goes on. The church calls those experiences *means of grace*. Means of grace are activities or experiences that help us to receive God's unconditional love. These activities do not earn God's love, approval, or favor. They simply put us in better positions to receive what God wants to give. I often use the illustration of a birthday party. The birthday girl does nothing to earn her presents, but she will have the best opportunity to receive them if she attends her party. The means of grace put us at the party where we receive God's gifts.

While there is an unlimited number of means of grace, there are five that are rooted in the life of Christ that have been effective throughout 2000 years of church history. They are known as the Instituted Means of Grace because Jesus instituted them. For the remainder of this chapter, we'll take a brief look at each of these five.

Holy Communion

In Luke 22, Jesus told the disciples that he "eagerly desired to eat this Passover" with them. He would go on to use the traditional Passover meal to institute the Lord's Supper, also known as Holy Communion or the Eucharist. It's easy to imagine this final meal as a graduation celebration to cap off three years of training as disciples. It's also been portrayed as a farewell meal where friends gather for one final night before going their separate ways. In both these examples, Jesus' eager desire makes sense, but there was something else going on.

This meal was hardly a celebration of the disciple's accomplishments. Their apprenticeships as disciples were more often characterized by failure than success. They couldn't heal people when Jesus thought they should. They couldn't feed the 5000 when Jesus told them to do it. Peter did walk on water, but then took his eyes off Jesus and nearly drowned. Two disciples actually asked to call down fire to burn up people they opposed. And, they were constantly bickering about which of them was the greatest, an argument that continued into the Last Supper! Jesus was not eager to celebrate the successes of the disciples at this meal.

Nor was it a fond farewell among loyal friends. While Jesus and the disciples were friends, the disciples were not yet loyal. During the meal, Jesus confirmed that one of the disciples would betray Him. Before the night was over, Peter would deny Him three times, and the others would desert Him and run for their lives. One disciple ran out of his clothes, streaking away from the Garden of Gethsemane to save his own hide.

Jesus was eager to share a meal with cowards, deserters, and a traitor. Jesus wanted to invite His enemies to the family table—and He still does. In most cultures, family forms around the dinner table. That fact is especially true in the church where the table is a symbol of the unconditional love of God. No one earns a seat at the table. No one deserves their place more than anyone else. Through Holy Communion, God offers grace, unconditional love, to whomever will come.

One of the oldest terms for the Trinity is *perichoresis* which can be translated "circle dance" (Theopedia). It's a beautiful image of Father, Son, and Holy Spirit eternally dancing together in a perfect loving relationship, each always giving honor and preference to the other. When Jesus offers us the bread and the cup, he is inviting us into the dance, not because we are good, but because God is good. Our morality doesn't earn us a seat at the table or get

us into the dance. Christianity is not about a list of
rules invented by ancient scholars, Queen Victoria, or
the preacher down the street. It's about a God who,
out of unfathomable love and goodness, invites the
least, the last, the lost, the failures, and even enemies
to the feast! Every time Holy Communion is served,
Christ renews that invitation. Every time we receive
bread and cup, we say, "Yes!"

Bible Study

Bible study is a valuable means of grace that
connects us with God, but the Bible, itself, is not
God! Throughout my life I've heard, "The Bible is the
Word of God," but John says, "The Word became
flesh and made his dwelling among us" (John 1:14a
NIV). So, is the Word of God Jesus, or is it a book?
And, if the Bible is the Word of God, then which
Bible? The protestant version has 66 books. The
Roman Catholic version has 73, and the Eastern
Orthodox Bible has 76 books. Which one should
Christians follow? Additionally, whenever the Bible
speaks about the Word of God, it cannot be speaking
about the complete text of the Bible, because,
obviously, it wasn't complete when those words were
written.

So, Bible study is important, but we should be
wise in our approach to our sacred book. We must
own the reality that, while inspired by God, it was
written by many different people over several
hundred years. Contextual difference must be taken
into consideration. Some of the Bible was written
while Israel was a super power. Other books were
written while Judah was in captivity, and still others
reflect times of Roman rule. The Bible includes

poetry, history, prophesy, and letters written to individuals and churches. Obviously, there is fallacy in treating poetry as if it were history and a personal letter as if it were prophesy. In one place, Paul admonishes women to be silent. In another, he says there is no difference between male and female. Inerrantists, who claim that the Bible is penned by the finger of God, have difficulty explaining such contradictions as well as scriptural instructions to execute homosexuals and disobedient children. The Bible is an invaluable tool in developing a relationship with God, but like any other tool, it can be used for evil or good.

Bible study that fosters a relationship with God is done against the backdrop of the Great Commandment. Jesus said that the entire law is contained in the commandment to love God and others. Any Bible reading that violates that law is an abuse of scripture. If Jesus is the true Word of God, then His words carry greater weight. All other scripture can be filtered through the words of Jesus.

With these cautions in mind, I will offer three simple guidelines to assist in Bible study. First, begin with prayer. God will help us understand the scriptures. "But the Advocate, the Holy Spirit, whom the Father will send in my name, will teach you all things and will remind you of everything I have said to you" (John 14:26 NIV). Part of the role of the Holy Spirit in our lives is to teach us the truth, both in the Bible and in life. Before trying to discern the meaning of the text, it's wise to ask for God to open our minds. This prayer helps us avoid the danger of reading our assumptions into the text. If I assume God opposes my enemies, then I will miss the meaning of Jesus' command to love my enemies in Matthew 5:44. Prayer helps us to move beyond our biases to hear what God wants us to know from the text.

Secondly, it's better to read for content than for volume. There are many plans available to help you "Read the Bible Through in a Year," and they're mostly unhelpful. The reading schedule they require is very ambitious if you stay on schedule. If you miss a day or two, it's almost impossible to catch up. Additionally, in an effort to complete the task of the daily reading, it's easy to miss the meaning of the text. Trying to read the whole Bible on schedule reminds me of the timed reading tests my daughter, Olivia, had to take in first grade. The teacher graded her on the number of words she could read in a minute, but when my wife and I asked her what she had read, she couldn't tell us. She sped through the words without catching the meaning. The same can happen with ambitious Bible reading plans.

Instead, I encourage people to read until they've heard from God. Pick a starting point and read until a verse or a passage speaks to you and your life situation. Sometimes, God speaks in the first verse you read. Another time, you read a passage before you've heard from God, and sill another time, you might read one or more chapters. The volume is not the objective, rather it's hearing from God that's important.

Thirdly, in Bible study, it's important to read for both information and transformation. There's much helpful information in the Bible. Christ followers should familiarize themselves with the stories of Jesus' birth, teachings, miracles, death, and resurrection. There are hundreds of important facts in the Bible, and it's helpful to learn them, but knowing facts is not sufficient. Bible reading should transform us. We should be different because of what we read. In this book, I've attempted to teach you the Great Commandment, to love God and others. Perhaps you've learned it. Maybe you can recite the words. You've learned the information. The words have transformed you when you demonstrate love to God and neighbor, when you act generously toward the person you don't like. Information is easy. Transformation is challenging and will require God's help.

Prayer

Sometimes, we use our prayers to treat God like Santa Claus or the butler. Prayer time is consumed with requests and commands. "God, please help me get debt free, and heal my Uncle Joe." Of course, Jesus tells us that we should ask for what we need, but requests shouldn't be the primary reason for prayer. Oswald Chambers reminds us in *My Utmost for His Highest* that the purpose of prayer is not answers but union with Christ. Through prayer, we develop a relationship with God that extends far beyond a divine "to do list." Largely absent from prayer in the western church is time for listening. Prayer is a two-way conversation.

We listen for God in meditation. One form of meditation focuses attention on an icon or some symbol that causes us to think of God. Silently gaze at a flower, or a cross, or a work of art, and wait for God to speak. The psalmist asserts, "The heavens declare the glory of God; the skies proclaim the work of his hands" (19:1 NIV). God is speaking through creation. The busyness of our lives makes it difficult, and sometimes impossible, for us to hear. This style of meditation allows us to listen.

Ignatian meditation is another form that helps us to hear God through the scriptures. In this method, you read a passage from the Bible and imagine yourself into the story. My favorite text for Ignatian meditation is the story of Jesus blessing the children (Luke 18:15-17). As I read the story, I imagine myself as one of the children. How does it feel to hear the disciples' rebuke? What's it like to hear Jesus defend me against their rebuke? How do those strong carpenter's hands feel as He picks me up? Does He toss me in the air? Tickle me? I imagine the coarseness of His beard and the sound of His voice. As I meditate on the story, I sense God's acceptance of me. After experiencing the role of one of the children, I might imagine myself as one of the disciples. What am I feeling as the kids push past me to get to the Master? What do I feel as Jesus rebukes me for my insensitivity towards children that He treasures? How does Jesus' correction feel? Am I willing for Him to correct me? Both roles help to shape me as a Christ follower.

Still another style of meditation invites us to simply become quiet before God and listen. This method is challenging in our noisy western culture. One Sunday morning before teaching on meditation, I decided to practice it on my drive to the church. Initially my focus on Christ was good, but less than one mile down the road I got distracted when I saw that gasoline prices had dropped. Noisy culture invades sacred time easily in our world. If you attempt to be quiet, expect stray ideas to wander frequently into your mind. When they do, a centering word will help clear your mind and return you to a state of quietness. The word you choose doesn't really matter. I often just say the name, Jesus. Early on, you will likely use your centering word every few seconds. This frequency is not a reason for frustration. With practice, you will require it less often. The quietness we experience in meditation makes us available to God. Impressions we receive during meditation may be God's gentle guidance to us for the day.

Of course, prayer does involve our speaking to God as well. You might repeat the Lord's Prayer or use it as an outline for your own prayer. Many people follow the acronym ACTS: adoration, confession, thanksgiving, and supplication. These are good methods, but the most helpful to me is talking to God with brutal honesty about whatever is going on in my life. I may be happy, sad, discouraged, or angry. I might be angry with God or be so frustrated that I don't even want to talk to God. Whatever I experience, I speak to God. It's the most honest conversation I ever have with anybody. I once told God that I would rather be playing on the computer than talking to Him! Such honesty always seems to lead me deeper into the depths of God than I'd been before. God and Moses spoke to one another as friends speak to each other (Exodus 33:11). Through prayer, we can hope for the same.

Fasting

I always assumed that fasting would lead to a spiritual high, a mountaintop experience. My first experience teaching fasting led me to see past those

111

expectations. Years ago, while leading a small group through various Christian disciplines, I introduced the topic of fasting and gave practical guidelines for group members to follow. I asked them to experiment with the discipline during the week and to share their experiences at our next meeting. All week long, I looked forward to hearing stories of euphoric experiences, of mystical breakthroughs in the spirit world, of burning bushes and flashes of lightening, of miraculously answered prayers, or at least stores of hearing the still, small voice of God. When my group convened the following week, I asked for people to share their experiences. One woman spoke up, "I just felt hungry!" Her honesty rattled me and deflated my enthusiasm. My disappointment must have been visible to the group! But, her response led me to explore fasting more thoroughly. She helped me develop a better understanding.

The purpose of fasting is not a mountaintop experience, nor is it a turbo booster for prayer. Fasting is an opportunity to tangibly demonstrate our love for God. Next to air, food is one of our strongest desires. During a fast, we set aside that strong desire to give preference to God. We demonstrate with our actions that God is even more important than our hunger. Fasting is a surrender of our wills to God's.

There are various styles and lengths of fasts. An absolute fast is abstaining from all food and liquid and is not advisable. A healthy human body can go for quite a while without food, but there are serious health implications with a lack of hydration. I discourage absolute fasts. A total food fast, involves abstaining from solid foods for a period of time while remaining hydrated. This style of fasting is generally safe for a healthy adult. If you have questions about your safety in fasting, please consult your physician. A partial fast involves giving up certain foods, usually for a longer period of time, as in giving up sweets or red meat for Lent. Regardless of the style, the intent is the same—to demonstrate that God is more important than our desires.

Just as the style is not critical, neither is the length or severity. I'm afraid that some people might think they impress God with the severity of their fasts, but many of the spiritual giants of the church never fasted for longer than 24 hours at a time. John Wesley, founder of the United Methodist Church, fasted for much of his life on Wednesdays and Fridays, but on neither day did his fast last a full 24 hours. The submission of our wills to God's through regular, moderate fasts will accomplish as much, or more, for our spiritual lives than extreme fasts. To learn more about the practical aspects of fasting, I recommend Richard Foster's work on the topic in *Celebration of Discipline*.

Fellowship or Accountability

My son Michael played high school football, which in Alabama is basically a year-round sport. During months when he didn't actually strap on the pads, the coaches expected him to lift weights and run. One summer, my family went away for two weeks during summer workouts. There was a gym at our destination, and I assured the coach that I would make Michael work out while we were away. The coach told me that those workouts would not count, that he would still be counted absent from those summer workouts. When I questioned this seemingly unfair policy, the coach explained that Michael would work out harder with the coaches watching him than he would alone. I couldn't argue that point.

Accountability develops us. God designed us for partnership.

Two are better than one,
> because they have a good return for their labor:

If either of them falls down,
> one can help the other up.

But pity anyone who falls
> and has no one to help them up.

Also, if two lie down together, they will keep warm.
> But how can one keep warm alone?

Though one may be overpowered,
> two can defend themselves.

A cord of three strands is not quickly broken.
(Ecclesiastes 4:9-12)

While it might be possible to live a spiritual life alone, it is much more likely for us to develop spiritually with the help of friends. Jesus sent the disciples out in pairs. Paul worked with Barnabas, and when that relationship broke down, he teamed up with Silas. If Paul needed companionship, most of us probably do. I've seen spiritual growth explode when people teamed up to hold one another accountable to these classical Christian disciplines.

In spite of the Biblical and historical evidence that accountability is vital, people still shy away from it. In my experience, the reason for apprehension is that people don't want to be chastised or abused for failure, especially since some failures are almost certain. I encourage positive accountability. Celebrate successes and be graceful with failures. When someone follows a discipline only two days out of seven, we celebrate the two days and set a reasonable goal for the next week to attempt to grow forward. Seldom is spirituality a consistent, "straight line" journey. Expect the path to be filled with both peaks and valleys. A spiritual friend helps keep you moving along the way.

Be selective in spiritual friends or guides. Consider someone who is mature in his or her relationship with God, who is secure in his or her own personality, and someone you are certain will work for your best interest. Be aware of anyone who makes lots of recommendations to try to "fix" you, and especially be aware of someone issuing divine directives. A divine directive is a claim to be speaking on behalf of God. If your spiritual guide says, "God told me that you need to fast more," end the relationship. It's abusive. A true spiritual friend will help you hear God but will never presume to speak on behalf of God.

Conclusion

This survey of the means of grace only barely skims the surface of ways that we can stay in love with God. The western church's focus on morality has seriously atrophied its experience of Christian mysticism. We have focused so much on controlling people's behavior that we have quenched the Spirit that would have given us life. As a result, people like Shannon who long for a spiritual connection are walking away. Their hunger is real, and those of us in the church should share it. May we lay down our obsession with rules and embrace life in the Spirit!

EPILOGUE

Thank you for taking this journey with me. Perhaps, if you've made it this far, you agree that moralism is a threat to genuine Christianity. Morality is not the path to God. For 2000 years, every generation has attempted to recast the Christian faith in its own image, usually to the advantage of the powerful. In the early years, the church demanded orthodoxy to unite the Roman Empire. In the Middle Ages, the church sold forgiveness to pay for its expensive building projects. During the Spanish Inquisition, it tortured people into allegiance to protect the power it wielded. For over 150 years, Queen Victoria inserted her own version of morality into Christian dogma so thoroughly that one can hardly tell the difference between the Queen's ideas and God's. In America, the church has used the Bible to support slavery and to subjugate women. It was highjacked in the 1800s by the Temperance Movement, and in the 20th and 21st Centuries it is the battleground for civil rights, and our descendants will decide whether the church took the faithful stand on that issue.

Through this tattered history, one clear conviction stands. Christ followers love God and love people. It's amazing that such a simple concept could be so severely twisted for two millennia. Still, for those who dare to listen to and follow that Great Commandment, life with God is possible. The Immoral Christian, unshackled from lists of Godless rules, rises from the ashes of the western church to unconditionally embrace God and people. The Immoral Christian is not a paradox but a lover of souls who has discovered the way that leads to life.

NOTES

Chapter One

Altman, Lawrence K. "Study Finds That
      Teenage Virginity Pledges Are
      Rarely Kept." *The New
      York Times*. 10 March 2004.
      https://www.nytimes.com/2004/03/10/us/stu
      dy-finds-that-teenage-virginity-pledges-are-
      rarely-kept.html.

Barna, George & David Kinnaman.   *Churchless*.
Tyndale, 2014.

Blakley, William Adamson. *The American
      State Papers: Bearing on Sunday
      Legislation*. Religious Liberty
      Association: Washington D. C.,
      1911.

*The Blue Laws of New Haven Colony:
      Usually Called Blue Laws of
      Connecticut; Quaker Laws
      of Plymouth and Massachusetts; Blue Laws
      of New York, Maryland, Virginia, and South
      Carolina. First Record of Connecticut;
      Interesting Extracts from Connecticut
      Records; Cases of Salem Witchcraft;
      Charges and Banishment of Rev. Roger
      Williams, &c.; and Other Interesting and
      Instructive Antiquities.* Case, Tiffany &
      Company, 1838.

Manning, Kathleen. "What is the History of
    Marriage?" *U. S. Catholic: Faith in
    Real Life*. Vol. 77, No. 11.
    November 2012.

                    Chapter Two
https://archive.org/stream/jstor-
    3154607/3154607_djvu.txt

Makutima, Adolfo. *My Philosophy.* Author
    House, 2014.

Manning, Kathleen. "What is the History of
    Marriage?" U. S. Catholic: Faith in
    Real Life. Vol. 77, No. 11.
    November 2012.

Owen, Helen L. "When Did the Catholic
    Church Decide Priests Should Be
    Celibate?"
    *Columbian College of Arts and
    Sciences: History News Network*. October
    2001.
    https://historynewsnetwork.org/article/696

Price, Richard M. "Celibacy and Free Love
    in Early Christianity." *Theology &
    Sexuality*. Vol. 12, No. 2. Sage:
    London, 2006.

Schneider, Mary R. "The Ancient Tradition
    of Clerical Celibacy."

CatholicCulture.Org.
https://www.catholicculture.org/culture/libra
ry/view.cfm?recnum=7663

Signpost 02.
https://signposts02.wordpress.com/2011/10/
08/a-short-history-of-christian-marriage

Chapter Four
Sprinkle, Preston. "What the Bleep Does the
Bible Say About Profanity?"
https://www.prestonsprinkle.com/blogs/theo
logyintheraw/2016/8/29/what-the-bleep-
does-the-bible-say-about-profanity.

Chapter Five
Conlin, Joseph R. *The American Past: A
Survey of American History.*

Harris, Robert R. "Against Moderation."
The New York Times. 6 May 2007.
https://www.nytimes.com/2007/05/0
6/books/review/Harris.t.html.

Lee, Barney. http://www.1timothy4-
13.com/files/teach/reasons.html.

Porter, Ebenezer. "The Fatal Effects of
Ardent Spirits." T. C. Strong, 1899.

Chapter Eight
Barna, George & David Kinnaman.
Churchless. Tyndale, 2014.

Chapter Ten
Theopedia.
https://www.theopedia.com/Perichoresis.

ABOUT THE AUTHOR

Kevin and his wife, Melissa, live in Tuscaloosa, AL where he serves as senior pastor of Forest Lake United Methodist Church. He received his BA from the University of Alabama, his Master of Divinity from Memphis Theological Seminary, and his Doctor of Ministry from Asbury Theological Seminary. Kevin and Melissa have three children: Michael, Katherine, and Olivia, and one daughter-in-law, Katherine's wife, Hannah. Kevin and Melissa enjoy family game nights, movies, cruising, and University of Alabama sporting events. Roll Tide!

For speaking engagements, contact Kevin at DoctorK223@gmail.com

Made in the USA
Monee, IL
07 July 2026

56550188R00075